Myth vs Reality

Exposing Falsehoods of Our Time

Alexander C

We'd love to hear from you! Your reviews help others discover the fun and fascinating world of myth-busting. Please take a moment to share your thoughts and leave a review on Amazon. Your feedback is greatly appreciated and helps spread the truth!

Copyright © 2024 by Alexander C

All rights reserved. No part of this publication may be reproduced, distributed, or transmitted in any form or by any means, including photocopying, recording, or other electronic or mechanical methods, without the prior written permission of the publisher, except in the case of brief quotations embodied in critical reviews and certain other noncommercial uses permitted by copyright law. ISBN: 9798329215236

"To my son, who fills my heart with joy each and every day."

Contents

Health and Medicine Myths — 13
Sugar Makes Kids Hyper — 14
Detox Diets Remove Toxins from the Body — 15
Toilet Seats Are the Dirtiest Things You Touch — 16
Eating at Night Makes You Fat — 17
Cracking Your Knuckles Causes Arthritis — 18
Shaving Hair Makes It Grow Back Thicker — 19
Reading in Dim Light Ruins Your Eyesight — 20
You Can Catch a Cold by Being Cold — 21
We Only Use 10% of Our Brain — 22

Food Myths — 25
Carrots Improve Your Night Vision — 26
MSG is Bad for You — 28
Microwaving Plastic Releases Harmful Chemicals — 30
Avoid Eggs Because of the Cholesterol — 31
Microwaving Food Zaps the Nutrients Out — 33
Spicy Food Causes Ulcers — 34
Eating Turkey Makes You Drowsy — 35
You Can Burn Off Alcohol by Sweating in a Sauna — 37
Chocolate Causes Acne — 39

Historical Myths — 41
Napoleon Was Short — 42
Marie Antoinette Said "Let Them Eat Cake" — 43
Vikings Wore Horned Helmets — 45
Columbus Discovered America — 46

Witches Were Burned at the Stake in Salem	47
The Great Wall of China Is Visible From Space	48
Lady Godiva Rode Naked Through Coventry	49
Albert Einstein Failed Math	50
The Iron Maiden Was a Medieval Torture Device	51
Paul Revere Shouted "The British Are Coming!"	52
Space Myths	**53**
There's No Gravity in Space	54
Humans Explode in Space Without a Suit	56
Black Holes Are Cosmic Vacuums	57
Astronauts Feel the Heat of the Sun in Space	58
Mercury Is the Hottest Planet Because It's Closest to the Sun	59
The Moon Has a Dark Side	60
Space Is a Complete Vacuum	61
Animal Myths	**63**
Ostriches Stick Their Heads in the Sand When Scared	64
Goldfish Have a Three-Second Memory	65
Bats Are Blind	66
Dogs Sweat by Salivating	67
Camels Store Water in Their Humps	68
Touching a Baby Bird Will Make Its Mother Reject It	69
Frogs Will Stay in Water As It Slowly Heats to Boiling	70
Elephants Are Afraid of Mice	71
Sharks Don't Get Cancer	72
A Cat's Purring Always Means It's Happy	73
Technology Myths	**75**

More Megapixels Mean Better Photos	76
Macs Can't Get Viruses	78
Incognito Mode Means You Are Invisible Online	80
Leaving Your Phone Plugged in Overnight Kills the Battery	82
Private Browsing Protects You From Hackers	84
More Bars on Your Phone Means Better Service	86
You Shouldn't Charge Your Phone Until It's Completely Dead	88
Using a Cell Phone at a Gas Station Can Cause an Explosion	90
You Need to Defragment Your SSD	92
Closing Apps on Your Phone Saves Battery	93
Psychological Myths	**95**
Left-Brained People Are Logical, Right-Brained People Are Creative	96
You Can Learn While You Sleep	98
You Only Have Five Senses	100
Opposites Attract	102
IQ Is Fixed and Determines Success	104
Mental Illness Is Rare	106
All Therapy Involves Lying on a Couch Talking About Your Childhood	107
Antidepressants Make You Happy All the Time	109
Weather Myths	**111**
Lightning Never Strikes the Same Place Twice	112
Tornadoes Always Move in the Same Direction	114
Hot Water Freezes Faster than Cold Water	116
Clouds Are Weightless	118

Heat Lightning is Different from Regular Lightning	119
Cows Lie Down When It's About to Rain	121
Hail Only Falls in the Summer	122
Snow is White	123
Survival Myths	**125**
You Can Suck Out Snake Venom	126
Moss Always Grows on the North Side of Trees	127
Rub Frostbitten Skin to Warm It Up	128
You Can Drink Your Own Pee in a Survival Situation	130
If You're Stabbed, Pull the Knife Out	132
Punch a Shark in the Nose to Escape an Attack	133
Playing Dead Will Save You from a Bear Attack	134
Running in a Zigzag Pattern Escapes Alligators	136
Cacti Are a Reliable Water Source	137
Parenting Myths	**139**
Picking Up a Crying Baby Spoils Them	140
You Have to Childproof Everything or Disaster Will Strike	141
TV Turns Kids into Zombies	143
Good Parents Never Get Angry	145
If Your Child Misbehaves, You're a Bad Parent	147
Parents Must Entertain Their Kids 24/7	149
Perfect Parents Exist	151
Babies Should Be on a Strict Schedule	152
Economic Myths	**155**
Trickle-Down Economics Always Works	156
All Debt is Bad	158

Printing More Money Solves Economic Problems	160
The Stock Market Reflects the Economy	162
Taxes Are Always Too High	164
Gold is the Safest Investment	166
Buying is Always Better than Renting	168
Economic Growth Can Continue Forever	170
Rich People Don't Pay Taxes	172
Automotive Myths	**175**
Red Cars Get More Speeding Tickets	176
Premium Gas Improves Performance in All Cars	177
SUVs Are Safer Than Smaller Cars	179
Manual Transmissions Get Better Fuel Economy	180
You Should Warm Up Your Car Before Driving	181
Controversial Myths	**183**
Vaccines Cause Autism	184
Climate Change is a Hoax	186
5G Technology Causes Health Issues	188
The Earth is Flat	190
Homeopathy is Effective	192
The Moon Landing Was Faked	194

"Truth with a Twist: Debunk, Laugh, Learn!"

Welcome to the ultimate guide to debunking the everyday myths that have crept into our lives like uninvited guests at a dinner party. If you've ever been told that cracking your knuckles will give you arthritis, or that you only use 10% of your brain, then you, my friend, have encountered the wild world of myths. In this book, we're setting out on a myth-busting adventure that's part science, part history, and all fun. Why myths, you ask? Because they're everywhere, stubbornly clinging to our collective consciousness like gum to a shoe. They spread faster than the latest internet challenge, and just like those challenges, they often leave us scratching our heads, wondering, "Is that really true?" Spoiler alert: It's usually not. Our journey will take us through a variety of categories, each more fascinating than the last. From medical myths that make your grandma's advice sound like it came from a medieval physician, to food myths that could make you question your next meal, we'll tackle them all. We'll explore space myths that make sci-fi movies seem like documentaries and parenting myths that'll have you laughing (and nodding) in recognition. But this isn't just about tearing down falsehoods. It's about celebrating the truth and marveling at the real wonders of our world. Plus, who doesn't love a good laugh while learning? Expect a lot of *"Aha!"* moments, mixed with chuckles and maybe the occasional guffaw as we navigate the murky waters of misinformation.

So grab your curiosity, pack your sense of humor, and let's embark on this myth-busting expedition together. Whether you're a skeptic, a believer, or somewhere in between, there's something in here for you. After all, the truth might be stranger than fiction, but it's also a whole lot more fun.

Let the debunking begin!

Disclaimer

The information provided in this book is intended for educational and entertainment purposes only. While every effort has been made to ensure the accuracy of the content, the author and publisher make no representations or warranties of any kind with respect to the completeness, accuracy, reliability, suitability, or availability of the information contained herein. Any reliance you place on such information is strictly at your own risk. The author and publisher are not responsible for any errors or omissions, or for any loss or damage of any kind incurred as a result of using the information in this book. This book is not intended to replace professional advice or consultation in any field, including but not limited to medical, legal, financial, or psychological matters. Always seek the advice of a qualified professional with any questions you may have regarding a specific issue or condition. The myths debunked in this book are based on current scientific understanding and historical research as of the publication date. Science and historical perspectives are constantly evolving, and new discoveries may alter the context or understanding of certain topics. The author and publisher are not liable for any changes in information or new developments that may arise after the publication of this book. In short, this book is here to inform and entertain. Laugh, learn, and enjoy, but use your own judgment and consult experts when needed. Happy myth-busting

Health and Medicine Myths

Sugar Makes Kids Hyper

Myth: Give a kid a cookie, and they turn into a tiny tornado.

Reality: Despite parents' testimonials at birthday parties worldwide, science begs to differ. Multiple studies, including those as sweet as the treats themselves, have found no consistent link between sugar and hyperactivity in children. In fact, the idea that sugar causes hyperactivity might be more about expectation than biochemistry. A double-blind study found that when parents think their kids have consumed sugar (even when they haven't), they perceive their children as more hyperactive. That's right, the mere idea of sugar parents into keen observers of chaos! Sweet Fact: The notion likely started from a misinterpretation of diet affecting behavior in conditions like ADHD, but no direct freeway from sugar intake to hyper zoomies exists. It could indeed be that the excitement of events where sugary treats are plentiful (think parties, holidays, and any place where adults wear funny hats) is what's actually energizing the kids.

Detox Diets Remove Toxins from the Body

Myth: Drink these mysterious shakes to cleanse your inner tube!

Reality: Your body isn't a medieval dungeon that needs a magical potion to flush out the bad spirits. In fact, you're equipped with some pretty nifty natural detoxifiers, your liver and kidneys. These organs are like the unsung heroes of a clean-up crew, tirelessly filtering out the gunk from what you eat, drink, and breathe every day. The liver metabolizes drugs and breaks down substances to make them less harmful, while the kidneys filter your blood to remove waste and balance bodily fluids. So, before you spend a fortune on detox shakes that claim they'll "revitalise your essence" or "purify your soul," remember that your body is already doing a stellar job at keeping things tidy. Drinking plenty of water, eating a balanced diet rich in fruits, vegetables, and whole grains, and getting regular exercise are all your body really needs to keep its detox systems running smoothly. And let's be honest, a broccoli and beet smoothie sounds less appealing than a balanced meal followed by a nice stroll or a good night's sleep!

Toilet Seats Are the Dirtiest Things You Touch

Myth: Public toilets are a germaphobe's nightmare.

Reality: Brace yourself for a shocking plot twist in the world of germs! While public toilet seats might get a bad rap as the villains of hygiene, they're surprisingly not the champions in the germ Olympics. In fact, objects like your smartphone screen or the innocent-looking kitchen sponge are teeming with more bacteria than your average toilet seat. Here's the scoop: Toilet seats get a regular scrub-down, making them less hospitable for bacteria. Meanwhile, your smartphone collects germs from every surface it touches and every hand that swipes it. And the kitchen sponge? It's a five-star resort for bacteria, soaking up food particles and moisture, the perfect combo for microbes to throw a bacteria bonanza. So, the next time you flinch at the sight of a public restroom, remember that the real microbial mosh pit is likely in your pocket or your sink!

Eating at Night Makes You Fat

Myth: Midnight snacks go straight to your hips.

Reality: Picture calories as tiny, clueless tourists: They don't have watches, can't tell time, and certainly don't care what time it is when they arrive. Weight gain hinges on the simple equation of calories in versus calories out, not the clock. So, if you consume more calories than you burn, whether they're from a moonlit rendezvous with a bowl of ice cream or a sunlit date with a doughnut, you'll gain weight. This whole notion that eating at night sends calories straight to your waistline probably comes from our tendency to choose less than-healthy snacks and overindulge when the stars are out. After all, few people reach for celery sticks at midnight, it's those seductive, calorie-packed snacks that whisper sweet nothings after dark. If your late-night cheeseburger is part of your total calorie count for the day and doesn't push you into excess, it's no more sinister than its daytime counterpart. Keep track of what you eat over 24 hours; your waistline isn't keeping a bedtime diary!"

Cracking Your Knuckles Causes Arthritis

Myth: Every pop of the knuckles is a step toward becoming a stiff robot.

Reality: Relax, you're not turning into the Tin Man from Oz. Knuckle cracking doesn't cause arthritis, your bones aren't filing a noise complaint! The satisfying pop you hear when you crack your knuckles is simply gas bubbles bursting in the synovial fluid that lubricates your joints. Here's how it works: When you pull, bend, or twist your fingers, you create negative pressure within the joint. This pressure change causes the dissolved gases in the synovial fluid (mainly nitrogen, oxygen, and carbon dioxide) to form bubbles. The pop is the sound of those bubbles bursting, not your joints screaming for mercy. So, go ahead and crack those knuckles without fear of turning into a creaky automaton. You might annoy your friends, but your joints are just fine with it. In fact, knuckle-cracking aficionados, your hands are simply enjoying a mini symphony of bubble pops. Just be prepared for the occasional side-eye from your non-cracking companions!

Shaving Hair Makes It Grow Back Thicker

Myth: Shave your legs, and you'll soon be a woolly mammoth!

Reality: Don't worry, shaving your hair won't turn you into the Yeti's long-lost cousin. Here's how it really works: When you shave, you're slicing off the hair at the surface of the skin. This gives the hair a blunt tip, which can feel coarser or thicker as it grows out. But this new hair isn't any thicker, darker, or faster-growing than before. It just feels that way because the sharp edge of the shaved hair is like a prickly little porcupine, not the soft, tapered end you get with natural growth. Think of it this way: Imagine you're cutting a tree. When you chop off the top, the stump left behind isn't thicker than the tree was, it's just a flat cut. The tree isn't plotting revenge, growing back with extra branches to make you work harder. Your hair is the same; it's not coming back with a vendetta. It's simply doing its usual thing, one hair follicle at a time. So, the next time you hear someone say that shaving will turn you into Bigfoot, you can laugh it off. Your hair follicles don't have the energy for a rebellion, they're just trying to keep up with your grooming routine. Shave away, and rest easy knowing you're not one step closer to joining the cast of a mythical creature documentary!

Reading in Dim Light Ruins Your Eyesight

Myth: Reading in low light turns you into Mr. Magoo.

Reality: Okay, let's set the scene: You're engrossed in a thrilling novel, the lighting's a bit dim, and your eyes are working overtime. Now, your eyes might get tired and give you a bit of a grumble, but they're not going to throw in the towel and demand prescription glasses just because of a few low-lit chapters. Here's the scoop: Your eyes have these incredible muscles that control the lens and pupils, adjusting to different light levels faster than a teenager can text. In dim light, your pupils dilate to let in more light, and your eye muscles work harder to focus. This can lead to eye strain, making your eyes feel like they've run a marathon, but it's a temporary condition. Imagine your eyes are tiny gym enthusiasts. When you read in dim light, it's like they're doing a few extra reps at the gym. They might be sore afterwards, but after some rest (and maybe a good night's sleep), they bounce back ready for more. There's no permanent damage happening here, just a temporary workout.

You Can Catch a Cold by Being Cold

Myth: Step outside with wet hair, and you'll catch your death!

Reality: The idea that you can catch a cold from being cold is as sturdy as a house of cards in a windstorm. Colds are caused by viruses, not by chilly weather or your wet mop of hair after a shower. These viruses (over 200 different types can cause a cold) hitch a ride from person to person through droplets in the air, sneezed or coughed out by someone already infected, or through direct contact. When it's cold outside, we tend to huddle indoors, sharing space and, unfortunately, germs, making it seem like the cold weather is to blame. It's not the actual cold that's the culprit but our response to it, packing into warm, enclosed spaces where viruses dance from one host to another more easily. So, while wearing a hat might keep you warm, it won't ward off the common cold unless it's made of hand sanitizer-soaked wool. Go ahead, brave the cold with your hair damp if you like living on the edge; just avoid the actual sick people plotting against your immune system.

We Only Use 10% of Our Brain

Myth: Legend has it that 90% of your brain is just loafing around.

Reality: This myth suggests that if only we could tap into that lazy 90%, we'd be out here moving objects with our minds and solving equations faster than a speeding bullet. But, spoiler alert: it's just not true. Brain scans like fMRI (functional Magnetic Resonance Imaging) and PET (Positron Emission Tomography) show that we use virtually every part of our brain, and most of it is active almost all the time. Imagine your brain is an office, but instead of a few people working while everyone else naps under their desks, it's more like a bustling hive of constant activity. Even when you're binge-watching your favorite show or pondering what toppings to get on your pizza, your brain is on full alert, coordinating thoughts, processing images, managing bodily functions, and sometimes, even helping you remember where you left your keys. Neuroscientists have debunked the 10% myth countless times. For example, activities like reading, solving problems, and even daydreaming light up different regions of the brain. If 90% of your brain were truly idle, it would likely shrivel up from disuse, like an unused muscle. Thankfully, evolution didn't design us that way. Every lobe and cortex is doing something, whether it's controlling movement, processing sensory information, or keeping your heart beating while you decide between pepperoni or mushrooms. So, why does this myth persist? Maybe it's the allure of untapped potential or the Hollywood trope of suddenly accessing superhuman abilities. But the reality is just as fascinating. Your brain is a marvel of efficiency and complexity, a 24/7 multitasker that makes you, well, you.

So, the next time someone trots out the 10% myth, you can confidently tell them, *"My brain is a full-time worker, not a part-time dreamer!"* And then maybe show off by remembering all your pizza order details without writing them down. Energy Hog: Your brain gobbles up about 20% of your body's energy. If 90% were napping, that would be like leaving the lights on all day in an empty mansion, wasteful and unlikely given our brain's efficiency.

Food Myths

Carrots Improve Your Night Vision

Myth: Eat carrots and you'll soon be seeing like a cat in a closet.

Reality: Imagine munching on a carrot and instantly transforming into a nocturnal superhero. Tempting, right? Unfortunately, it's not that simple. While carrots are packed with beta-carotene, which your body converts into vitamin A, a nutrient crucial for maintaining healthy vision, they won't grant you feline night vision superpowers. Here's the twist: this myth actually has a colorful backstory from World War II. The British Royal Air Force started spreading the tale that their pilots had superb night vision because they ate a lot of carrots. The truth? They were using a top-secret technology called radar to spot enemy aircraft in the dark. But rather than reveal this game-changing tech to the enemy, they credited the humble carrot for their nocturnal prowess. It was like saying, "No, we're not using sophisticated tech to beat you; we just have a lot of really enthusiastic rabbit impersonators!" So, while chomping on carrots will indeed help keep your vision sharp (thanks to vitamin A), it won't turn your eyes into high-beam headlights. You won't be reading in the dark or spotting ninjas in the shadows. But hey, they're still great for your overall health, and your mom wasn't completely off base when she told you to eat them. Plus, they're a lot cheaper than night-vision goggles! In short, keep eating your carrots, they're good for you, but don't expect to start moonlighting as a superhero in the dark. That's a job best left to radar, cats, and comic book characters.

MSG is Bad for You

Myth: MSG will make your brain buzz and your body bloat.

Reality: MSG will make your brain buzz and your body bloat like a balloon in a parade. Reality: Let's clear the air, MSG (monosodium glutamate) has been cast as the villain in many a dining drama, but the plot thickens beyond these myths. MSG is essentially a flavor enhancer that brings out the umami, the so-called fifth taste that makes everything from chips to chicken soup taste like a chef kissed it. Chemically, it's just sodium and glutamate (which is a type of amino acid found naturally in many tasty foods like tomatoes and cheese).Now, why the bad rep? Back in the 1960s, aetter to a medical journal linked a variety of symptoms to Chinese restaurant food, coining it "Chinese Restaurant Syndrome." However, extensive research since then, including studies by the FDA and other international food safety authorities, has found no definitive evidence that links MSG to these symptoms when consumed in typical amounts. It turns out, you're more likely to feel "symptoms" from overeating than from MSG sprinkled in your meal. So, if MSG is in the script, think of it as the misunderstood character who actually enhances the plot without hogging the spotlight. Your brain won't buzz any more than it would from eating parmesan, and your body won't bloat unless you're really going overboard on your snack script. In short, MSG isn't the culinary villain it's been cooked up to be; it's just another cast member in the delicious drama of dining.

Microwaving Plastic Releases Harmful Chemicals

Myth: Microwaves turn plastic into a toxic tumbleweed.

Reality: While the idea of your microwave morphing plastics into a miniature Chernobyl is dramatic, it's not entirely accurate. Not all plastics are secret supervillains waiting to leach chemicals into your spaghetti bolognese. In the world of plastics, there are heroes and villains. The heroes in this saga are the microwave-safe plastics. These champions are specially designed to handle the heat without sweating, or melting down, chemicals into your food. When plastics are labeled "microwave-safe," they've passed rigorous testing to ensure they can take the heat without releasing harmful substances. These plastics are made to withstand high temperatures generated by microwaves without breaking down. On the flip side, non-microwave-safe plastics might release chemicals like BPA or phthalates when they're heated, not because they're evil by nature, but because they weren't cast for this particular role.

Avoid Eggs Because of the Cholesterol

Myth: Eggs are cholesterol bombs waiting to explode your heart.

Reality: Hold onto your egg cups, because this is going to get egg-citing! For years, eggs were cast as the cholesterol villain in the breakfast saga, blamed for plotting against our arteries. Yes, one large egg packs about 186 mg of cholesterol, which sounds like it's just waiting to wreak havoc on your cardiovascular system. But plot twist: the latest scramble of studies shows that the cholesterol found in food has less impact on your blood cholesterol levels than we once feared. Here's the sunny-side up truth: your liver is the maestro behind most of the cholesterol in your body, and it adjusts production based on how much you consume. When you eat more cholesterol-rich foods like eggs, your liver simply produces less cholesterol itself. So for most people, chowing down on eggs doesn't lead to a spike in the villainous LDL (low-density lipoprotein) cholesterol that can clog arteries.

Moreover, eggs are like the multivitamins of the food world. They're packed with high-quality protein, vitamin B12, riboflavin, and phosphorus, and let's not forget choline, a brain-boosting nutrient that's doing the cha-cha in the yolk. They're also one of the few food sources of vitamin D, which is like sunshine you can eat. In summary, unless your healthcare provider advises you otherwise due to specific health conditions, eggs can be part of your "egg-cellent" diet. So, crack them open with less fear and more culinary ambition! It's time to let those egg puns, and nutrients, fly!

Microwaving Food Zaps the Nutrients Out

Myth: Every time you microwave, your food waves a white flag, surrendering its nutrients in abject defeat.

Reality: Hold on to your apron! Contrary to the popular culinary myth, microwaving your food doesn't turn it into nutritional dust. In fact, microwaving can be like a spa retreat for your veggies, keeping them fresher and more nutrient-packed than other cooking methods. Here's why: Microwaving uses electromagnetic waves that heat up the water molecules in food, causing them to vibrate and quickly heat up the food from the inside out. This fast-cooking superpower means there's less time for nutrients to run off and hide, unlike boiling, where vitamins can jump ship intothe water and go down the drain. Plus, because you're using minimal water, water-soluble nutrients (like vitamin C and several B vitamins) don't get diluted as much as they do when you're simmering veggies in a pot.

Spicy Food Causes Ulcers

Myth: Spicy food is the fire starter of stomach ulcers

Reality: Spicy food is like inviting a flamethrower to a paper factory, sure to start an ulcer. Reality: Time to extinguish this fiery myth! Ulcers aren't sparked by your love for jalapeños and habaneros. Instead, most stomach ulcers are caused by a less spicy culprit: a bacterium known as Helicobacter pylori (H. pylori), or by the prolonged use of NSAIDs (non-steroidal anti-inflammatory drugs), like ibuprofen and aspirin. These are the real heat behind the burn, eating away at the stomach's protective lining until, voila! An ulcer is born. While spicy foods can make an existing ulcer feellike a salsa dance on your insides, they're not the ones that roll out the red carpet for ulcers. They might irritate an already sensitive stomach lining, but they don't cause the initial damage. So, if your gut's in good shape, diving into that spicy curry doesn't automatically RSVP you to the ulcer party. Keep the milk handy, not because you're preventing ulcers, but because sometimes that spice kicks back!

Eating Turkey Makes You Drowsy

Myth: Turkey is nature's sleeping pill.

Reality: Ah, the great Thanksgiving nap myth! The belief that turkey alone can knock you out faster than a late-night infomercial is a bit overcooked. Turkey does contain tryptophan, an amino acid that can be converted into serotonin and then melatonin, the hormone that helps regulate sleep. But here's the twist: turkey doesn't have more tryptophan than other common meats like chicken or beef. In fact, gram for gram, cheddar cheese and nuts have more tryptophan than turkey does. So why do you feel like curling up on the couch after that Thanksgiving feast? Blame it on the festive gluttony! When you devour a mountain of mashed potatoes, a sea of stuffing, and a parade of pies, your body has to work overtime to digest all that food. This process redirects blood flow to your digestive system, leaving your brain with less oxygen and energy, resulting in the post-meal drowsiness often mistaken for the turkey's hypnotic powers.

And let's not forget the carb coma. All those delicious carbs increase insulin production, which helps clear competing amino acids from your bloodstream, allowing tryptophan to enter the brain more easily. So, while the tryptophan from the turkey plays a small role, it's really the carbohydrate cavalry that's aiding and abetting your need for a nap. In other words, it's not just the turkey that's lulling you into dreamland, it's the entire Thanksgiving smorgasbord conspiring to make you sleepy. So, the next time someone blames the turkey, you can laugh and say, *"Nice try! It's the whole feast that's the culprit!"* Now, excuse me while I unbutton my pants and enjoy a well-earned snooze.

You Can Burn Off Alcohol by Sweating in a Sauna

Myth: Sweat it out in a sauna, and you'll be sober in no time.

Reality: Ah, if only sobering up was as easy as sweating it out in a sauna! Unfortunately, your liver didn't get the memo. The body metabolizes alcohol at a consistent rate, which is roughly one standard drink per hour. No amount of sweating, whether in a sauna or running a marathon, will speed up this process. Here's the deal: when you drink alcohol, it's absorbed into your bloodstream and then processed by your liver. The liver, being the hardworking organ it is, breaks down alcohol into acetaldehyde, then further into acetate, and finally into water and carbon dioxide, which your body can eliminate. This process takes time, more time than it takes to binge-watch your favorite show. Hitting the sauna might make you sweat buckets, but it's not the alcohol that's coming out, it's just water. And here's the kicker: spending too much time in the sauna while you're already dehydrated from drinking can actually make you feel worse, not better. Dehydration can intensify hangover symptoms like headache, dizziness, and fatigue. So, rather than emerging from the sauna as a sober, fresh cucumber, you're more likely to come out feeling like a wilted, overcooked veggie. So next time you think about sweating out the booze, remember: your liver is the real MVP, and it's working at its own pace, no matter how many steam rooms you visit. Better to hydrate, rest, and give your liver the time it needs to do its job. In the meantime, enjoy the sauna for relaxation, not as a magic cure for your bar tab!

Chocolate Causes Acne

Myth: Chocolate lovers are pimple magnets.

Reality: Good news for the chocoholics! While it's tempting to blame your skin's rebellious breakout on that bar of heavenly chocolate, science doesn't back up the guilt trip. The myth that chocolate causes acne is as outdated as flip phones. Dermatological research has struggled to find a concrete connection between chocolate consumption and increased acne. In fact, skin flare-ups are more closely tied to hormonal imbalances and bacteria battles raging on your face. Of course, like any good superhero story, chocolate isn't entirely off the hook, it could still influence your skin if you have specific sensitivities, but for most people, chocolate isn't the villain in the saga of spots. So, unless your dermatologist advises otherwise, feel free to indulge in your cocoa cravings. Remember, moderation is key, because while chocolate won't mess up your skin, it can still wage war on your waistline if you let it!

Historical Myths

Napoleon Was Short

Myth: Napoleon was a tiny tyrant.

Reality: Poor Napoleon! He's been the butt of short jokes for centuries, but in reality, he wasn't short at all, he was about 5'7", which was average height for a Frenchman of his era. So why the myth? Blame it on British propaganda, eager to belittle their formidable foe in more ways than one. Also, Napoleon surrounded himself with his Imperial Guards, a squad of giants handpicked for their towering presence, making him look like a hobbit in comparison. Imagine constantly posing with NBA players, suddenly, you're Frodo Baggins. The French measured height differently back then, using the French foot, which was longer than the British foot. When translated, his height got lost in conversion, shrinking him unfairly in historical records. So, while we've been chuckling at the idea of a vertically-challenged conqueror, the joke's actually on us. Napoleon's height wasn't the real issue; it was his ambition that was sky-high. He was busy conquering Europe, not reaching for the top shelf. Next time you think of Napoleon, remember: he was average height but an above-average overachiever.

Marie Antoinette Said *"Let Them Eat Cake"*

Myth: Marie Antoinette was a pastry-pushing monarch

Reality: This deliciously scandalous quote has stuck to Marie Antoinette like frosting on a croissant, but there's no evidence she ever uttered these infamous words. The phrase "Let them eat cake" was first attributed to her years after her death and was likely a case of political slander baked up to paint her as oblivious to the plight of the French people. The real scoop is that this line was floating around long before Marie Antoinette could even pronounce "croquembouche." The French philosopher Jean-Jacques Rousseau mentioned a similar quote in his autobiography when Marie was just a little girl, attributing it to a "great princess" who is still a mystery. Historians believe this was a way to smear her reputation, turning her into the historical equivalent of a reality TV villain, out of touch and dripping in decadence. Marie Antoinette, in reality, was more likely to have said, *"Let them eat brioche,"* if she was truly that clueless, but alas, even that is doubtful. She had her own issues trying to navigate the tumultuous political landscape and had enough on her plate without advocating for a national cake buffet. So, the next time someone brings up Marie Antoinette and her alleged cake suggestion, you can roll your eyes and say, *"That's just a historical croissant of a lie, filled with misinformation and baked to perfection by her political enemies."* And maybe have a slice of cake yourself, because unlike the myth, cake is always a good idea.

Vikings Wore Horned Helmets

Myth: Vikings sailed into battle sporting stylish horned headgear.

Reality: The image of a Viking sporting a horned helmet is about as accurate as a dragon in your backyard. Imagine trying to navigate a crowded longboat or a fierce melee with two giant horns on your head, it's a recipe for poking out an eye, and not just your enemy's! In truth, the horned helmet is a historical hiccup that gained traction during the 19th century, largely thanks to artists like Gustav Malmström and opera costumes designed for Richard Wagner's productions, which favored drama over historical accuracy. In reality, Viking helmets were typically made from iron and were conical shaped to deflect blows in battle. No horns, no hassle! Archaeologists have dug up many Viking helmets, and none have come accessorized with horns. This headgear was all about practicality, not flair, which means Vikings were more about protecting their brains than decorating their domes with cumbersome and impractical ornaments. So, the next time you picture a Viking, think less bull in a china shop and more skilled warrior with a sensible hat!

Columbus Discovered America

Myth: Christopher Columbus was the pioneer GPS of America.

Reality: Saying Columbus discovered America is like walking into a packed party and claiming you discovered it, surprise, the party was already in full swing and you're just late! Indeed, millions of indigenous people had been living in the Americas for thousands of years, making the continents anything but new or uncharted. Furthermore, Columbus wasn't even the first European to drop anchor on its shores. That credit likely goes to the Norse explorer Leif Erikson, who set up a temporary camp in what is now Newfoundland, Canada, around the year 1000 AD, nearly 500years before Columbus sailed the ocean blue in 1492. So, while Columbus did play a significant role in European engagement with the Americas, his "discovery" wasn't the GPS breakthrough in unexplored territory that early history lessons might have us believe. Columbus might have thought he was opening new navigation routes, but really, he was just late to a party that had started without him!

Witches Were Burned at the Stake in Salem

Myth: Salem's witches faced a fiery end.

Reality: The Salem Witch Trials, while a seriously grim chapter in history, didn't feature a single witch BBQ. Despite the fiery imaginations of Hollywood directors and creepy Halloween decorations, the truth is no accused witches met their end by fire in Salem. In 1692, the preferred method of dealing with those unfortunate souls accused of witchcraft in this Massachusetts town was far less cinematic but equally tragic, they were hanged. Nineteen accused witches were sent to the gallows, and one unlucky man was pressed to death under heavy stones for refusing to enter a plea. Meanwhile, others died in the cramped, dismal conditions of their prison cells. The whole "burning witches at the stake" thing was more of a European flair, a continental twist on oppression. So, while Salem was certainly no party, it wasn't the hot spot for witch burnings some think it was.

The Great Wall of China Is Visible From Space

Myth: Astronauts admire the Great Wall of China during their spacewalks.

Reality: Despite popular claims, the Great Wall of China isn't the cosmic landmark many think it is. In reality, it's quite challenging to spot from space with the naked eye. Why? Well, contrary to its name, the Great Wall isn't that great in width, it's relatively narrow, and its colors often blend in with the natural landscape, making it a master of camouflage. Even NASA astronauts have confirmed that spotting it from space is no small feat, requiring specific weather and lighting conditions. So, while you might imagine astronauts pointing out the Great Wall on a spacewalk, they'remore likely asking each other, "Can you see it? Because I sure can't!" It turns out, many man-made objects and structures are tricky to spot from that high up, and the Great Wall is no exception, it's less 'visible landmark' and more 'Where's Waldo?' of the ancient world.

Lady Godiva Rode Naked Through Coventry

Myth: Lady Godiva was the original naked protester.

Reality: Picture this: Lady Godiva, the patron saint of exhibitionists, galloping through Coventry with nothing but her flowing locks. Quite the tale, but historical accuracy might beg to differ. The story goes that Lady Godiva rode naked through the streets to convince her husband, the Earl of Mercia, to lower the oppressive taxes on her people. However, this spicy snippet of historical gossip didn't pop up until about a century after her supposed ride, written by a monk who probably enjoyed a good scandal as much as the next guy. The reality is that the tale likely evolved as a moral lesson, perhaps about sacrifice, nobility, or the power of a dramatic gesture. Over the centuries, Lady Godiva's story has been romanticised and embellished, turning her into a folklore hero. But as for historical documents or eyewitness accounts? As bare as Lady Godiva herself on her legendary ride.

Myth: Einstein was a mathematical dud before he was a genius.
Reality: Picture this: young Albert Einstein, not just passing math, but crushing it so hard that the numbers probably had to take a sick day. The myth that Einstein was a poor math student

Albert Einstein Failed Math

Myth: Einstein was a mathematical dud before he was a genius.

Reality: Picture this: young Albert Einstein, not just passing math, but crushing it so hard that the numbers probably had to take a sick day. The myth that Einstein was a poor math student is a wildly inaccurate rendition of his academic prowess. It stems from a misunderstanding or mistranslation of his early school records; when his family moved to Italy and he switched schools, the grading system was the opposite of the German one. An 'A' suddenly looked like an 'F', and confusion ensued like a poorly planned surprise party. In truth, Einstein was mastering differential and integral calculus before his seventeenth birthday, while most of us were still trying to figure out how many apples Janice ended up with if she started with five and ate two. The guy was practically a mathlete superhero, dealing with equations like they were mere side quests in his quest for scientific glory. So next time you hear someone say Einstein failed math, you can laugh knowing he was probably theorizing relativity while his peers were still working on not eating the paste.

The Iron Maiden Was a Medieval Torture Device

Myth: The Iron Maiden was the medieval equivalent of a bad hotel review: *"Terrible stay, would not recommend. Too stabby."*

Reality: The notorious Iron Maiden, often depicted in movies and museums as a medieval staple for punishment, was actually a sensational fabrication from later centuries. Think of it as the historical equivalent of clickbait! It's an iron cabinet designed to look like a human figure, outfitted with spikes on the inside, not something you'd want to use as a coat closet. However, this gruesome gadget was likely never used in medieval times as advertised. Its first verifiable mention and display didn't pop up until the 18th century, during a time when curators and historians were a bit too enthusiastic about demonstrating the barbarity of the "dark" ages. It was more about shock value and less about historical accuracy. They essentially created the medieval version of a horror movie prop to draw in crowds.

Paul Revere Shouted *"The British Are Coming!"*

Myth: Paul Revere was the original hype man for the American Revolution, yelling *"The British are coming!"* as he rode through the night.

Reality: Paul Revere, the midnight rider, wasn't out there doing his best town crier impression. In fact, shouting such a phrase would have been counterproductive and a bit silly, considering most colonists still identified as British. They'd be like, "Yes, and...?" Instead, Revere discreetly spread the word that "The Regulars are coming out," referring to the British troops (also known colloquially as Regulars). This phrase was a much-needed heads-up that the king's troops were mobilizing, and not a declaration of an intergalactic invasion. It was all very hush-hush; after all, yelling at the top of your lungs is a great way to get a musket ball invitation to your last supper. So, Revere's ride was more covert ops, less blockbuster announcement, keeping the revolutionaries one step ahead in their quiet game of colonial chess.

Space Myths

There's No Gravity in Space

Myth: Space is a zero-gravity amusement park.

Reality: Strap in, because we're not floating through this explanation! The myth that there's no gravity in space is as off-base as thinking a pizza can be a diet food if you eat it with a diet soda. In reality, gravity is everywhere, even in space. What astronauts experience isn't the absence of gravity; it's microgravity. This means gravity is still at play but at a much weaker level compared to what we feel on Earth. So, why the floating astronauts, you ask? Well, when spacecraft orbit the Earth, they are essentially in free fall towards the planet but moving forward so quickly that they keep missing it! Yes, they're perpetually falling around Earth, which creates the sensation of weightlessness. It's like if you were in an elevator and suddenly the cables snapped (let's hope not), you and the elevator would fall together, making you feel weightless inside. This continuous free fall in orbit is basically space's version of the endless trust fall exercise, except you're trusting physics, not a person who might get distracted by a text.

This microgravity environment allows astronauts to pull off those cool flips and eat floating M&Ms right out of the air, but it's all thanks to Earth's gravity still pulling on them, just from a much cosier, less bone-crushing distance. So next time you see an astronaut doing a somersault in space, remember, it's not magic, t's just physics with a sense of humor!

Humans Explode in Space Without a Suit

Myth: Astronauts without suits turn into space popcorn

Reality: The idea of humans exploding in space is a bit over the top, like something out of a bad sci-fi movie. In reality, the absence of atmospheric pressure in space does lead to some pretty wild effects on the human body, but exploding isn't one of them. Here's the less dramatic truth: the vacuum of space causes the water in your body to vaporize (since water boils at lower temperatures in lower pressures), leading to a rather uncomfortable swelling. But don't worry, you wouldn't balloon up like a Thanksgiving Day parade float. Your skin is surprisingly stretchy and tough, so it holds everything together. This swelling isn't your biggest problem though. The lack of oxygen would knock you unconscious in about 15 seconds, and you'd be on a one-way trip to the afterlife shortly thereafter. And let's not forget about the freezing temperatures and cosmic radiation, space is silently brutal! So, while your body would endure some pretty extreme conditions in space sans suit, you'd remain decidedly unexploded. Hollywood might be disappointed, but your skin is definitely relieved.

Black Holes Are Cosmic Vacuums

Myth: Black holes are the universe's own brand of vacuum cleaners, roaming around and sucking up galaxies.

Reality: The image of black holes as cosmic Roombas gobbling up galaxies in their path adds a bit of interstellar drama, but it's far from accurate. Black holes don't wander the cosmos vacuuming up stars and planets. Instead, they're more like cosmic sinkholes. They form when massive stars collapse under their own gravity at the end of their life cycles, creating a point in space with gravitational pull so strong that not even light can escape, hence the "black" in black hole. However, their gravitational pull works much like that of any other object in space: it affects things based on proximity and mass. If you replaced the sun with a black hole of equal mass, Earth and the other planets would continue orbiting it just as before, not sucked in but held by gravity's leash. It's only when you get too close, crossing the infamous 'event horizon,' that the escape becomes impossible. Think of it as the cosmic point of no return, like getting an invitation to a family reunion and realising you can't come up with a polite way to decline.

Astronauts Feel the Heat of the Sun in Space

Myth: Astronauts in space get to soak up the sun's rays like they're lounging on a beach in Hawaii.

Reality: Imagine space as the universe's most extreme beach, but without any air to actually feel the warmth of the sun. In space, there's no air to conduct or convect heat from the sun, meaning the sun's energy hits in the form of radiation. When astronauts are in direct sunlight, they can feel as if they're in an oven, with temperatures soaring over 250 degrees Fahrenheit. Conversely, in the shade, it can plummet to minus 250 degrees. Thankfully, their space suits aren't just snazzy fashion statements; they're highly sophisticated personal climate-controlled systems. These suits have layers designed to reflect solar radiation and systems to remove excess body heat, maintaining a "just right" Goldilocks zone. So, while astronauts might miss building sandcastles, at least they don't have to worry about reapplying SPF 50 every two hours!

Alexander C.

Mercury Is the Hottest Planet Because It's Closest to the Sun

Myth: Mercury must be steaming because it's lounging next to the solar grill.

Reality: You might think Mercury would win the solar system's "Hot Body" contest, given its prime real estate next to the sun, but it's actually Venus that takes the sizzling crown. Mercury, despite its proximity, experiences the most dramatic day-night temperature swings of any planet in our solar system. This is because it doesn't have a thick atmosphere to act as a cozy blanket, trapping heat. At night, temperatures on Mercury can plummet to minus 280 degrees Fahrenheit (-173 degreesCelsius), because all the sun's warmth it soaked up during the day just leaks back out into Meanwhile, Venus is swaddled in a thick, toxic blanket of carbon dioxide that traps heat through a runaway greenhouse effect, making it the ultimate winner in the interplanetary sauna stakes, with average surface temperatures a toasty 867 degrees Fahrenheit (464 degrees Celsius). So, Mercury might get more sun, but Venus knows how to keep the heat!

The Moon Has a Dark Side

Myth: The moon hides a mysterious dark side that never sees light.

Reality: Contrary to Pink Floyd's musings and common misconceptions, the moon's "dark side" isn't an angsty teenager hiding in the shadows, it gets just as much sunlight as the side we see. The term "dark" refers to our knowledge of it, not its lighting conditions. The moon is tidally locked with Earth, meaning it rotates on its axis in the same amount of time it takes to orbit Earth. This cosmic dance keeps one face, the "near side"permanently turned toward us, grinning with its seas and craters, while the "far side" remains out of view, shyly showing its features only to the cosmos. So, the far side isn't actually dark; it's just playing hard to get, revealing its sunlit surface to space voyagers and satellites that dare to venture around it. Think of it as the moon's version of "playing it cool" a celestial mystery by virtue of its modesty, not its lack of sunlight.

Alexander C.

Space Is a Complete Vacuum

Myth: Space is nothingness, just a complete vacuum.

Reality: Calling space a complete vacuum is like saying your bedroom is clean because you shoved everything under the bed. In reality, space, though a pretty good vacuum, isn't absolutely empty. It's filled with a smattering of cosmic confetti, particles, dust, and cosmic rays that never got the memo about empty space. Even in the vast voids between stars and planets, there are still a few rogue hydrogen atoms per cubic meter, proving that nature really does abhor a vacuum. So, while space might be the best vacuum we know (sorry, Dyson), it's more like a party venue after everyone's left, a bit of debris, some forgotten particles, and the cosmic rays still bouncing around.

Animal Myths

Ostriches Stick Their Heads in the Sand When Scared

Myth: Ostriches believe "out of sight, out of mind" is the best strategy when danger lurks.

Reality: Think about it, if ostriches really buried their heads in the sand, they'd have evolved to breathe through their feathers! The truth is, these birds don't engage in sand-surfing headfirst. What they're actually doing when they press their long necks and heads to the ground is trying their best to blend in. Given their size and the sparse cover in their natural habitats, this might be the best they can do at a ninja vanish. When a predator approaches, lying low is the ostrich's version of "playing it cool." Their plumage blends remarkably well with sandy soils and dry grasses. So, while it looks like they're trying to become ostrich-ostriches, they're just using their heads, literally, to use the ground as a sort of primitive invisibility cloak. Plus, from a distance, this behaviour might look like they've buried their heads in the sand, especially to the casual observer or someone without binoculars. But rest assured, they're fully aware of their surroundings and ready to spring up and leg it at speeds of up to 60 mph if the predator gets too close. So much for not knowing what's going on above ground!

Goldfish Have a Three-Second Memory

Myth: By the time they swim around their bowl, it's a brand-new world!

Reality: Surprise! Goldfish are not swimming Post-It notes with a short lifespan of memories. In reality, these little aquatic Einsteins pack more memory prowess than they get credit for. Research has shown that goldfish can remember things for up to five months, not just mere seconds. They're capable of distinguishing between different shapes, colors, and sounds. By using positive reinforcement, scientists and pet owners alike have trained goldfish to navigate mazes, push levers, and even perform impressive tricks like playing soccer or basketball in their aquatic arenas. This means that every time you pass by the fishbowl, your goldfish might actually be thinking, "Oh, it's YOU again," instead of, "Who the heck is that?" Their brainpower is strong enough to handle complex tasks, proving that these golden swimmers are more wizard than muggle in the memory department. So next time you think about upgrading your home security system, maybe just get a goldfish and train it to remember suspicious faces!

Bats Are Blind

Myth: Bats are the Mr. Magoo of the animal kingdom

Reality: Let's clear the air, bats are not blind, not even close! These winged wonders have a pretty nifty trick up their sleeve (or wing?): echolocation. This means they emit high-frequency sounds that bounce off objects and return to their super-sensitive ears, allowing them to create a sonic map of their surroundings. It's like having built-in sonar, a biological bat-nav if you will, which is handy for avoiding obstacles and zeroing in on the mosquitoes that you were just about to slap. But here's where it gets even cooler: bats can actually see as well. In fact, depending on the species, some bats have excellent night vision. Their eyes are well adapted to low-light conditions, much better than humans can ever hope to see in the dark, no night-vision goggles needed for these nocturnal navigators. They're basically the pilots of the animal kingdom, equipped with natural night vision and radar systems. So, while their eyesight might not be as sharp as, say, a hawk's during the day, they're perfectly suited for a moonlit flight through the forest. Next time you think about bats, picture them as the high-tech stealth bombers of nature, not bumbling, blind flyers!

Alexander C.

Dogs Sweat by Salivating

Myth: When your dog drools, it's trying to cool off its hot dog status.

Reality: Think of drooling as your dog's way of saying, *"Look how much I love that sausage,"* not, *"I'm overheating!"* While humans sweat it out through their entire skin when it's hotter than a jalapeño in a hot tub, dogs have a different cooling system. They do sweat, but you won't see them getting all sweaty like a gym buff. Instead, they sweat through their paw pads, which is about as effective as trying to air condition your house by opening just one window. But the real MVP of the canine cooling system? Panting. This is where dogs really get down to chill out business. When dogs pant, they evaporate moisture from their tongues, nasal passages, and the lining of their lungs, cooling themselves as air passes over the moist tissue. It's like having an internal fan that cranks up when things get too hot. Drooling, on the other hand, is more about managing delicious smells and tastes, or sometimes a bit of anxiety, basically, it's emotional sweat, not a cooling mechanism. So next time your dog starts panting at the park, they're not just trying to show off their impressive breathing skills, they're actually firing up their biological air-con!

Camels Store Water in Their Humps

Myth: Camels are just desert water tanks.

Reality: Think of a camel's hump as less of a water bottle and more of a packed lunch, or maybe a high-fat snack pack. These majestic desert navigators don't use their humps to store water as commonly believed, but rather they pack them with fat, which can be metabolised into water and energy during those long, food-scarce treks across the sand. When a camel munches down its meal, the body converts the food into fat, which is then stored in the hump. This fat reserve is incredibly efficient. When resources are low, the camel taps into this fat stash, breaking it down not just for energy but also releasing metabolic water, a byproduct of fat metabolism. It's like having a food processor that not only makes smoothies but also spits out water! So, essentially, a camel doesn't carry a water tank but rather a portable fatty diner that cleverly churns out water when the rest of the landscape is just sun and sand. This system allows camels to go for weeks without drinking, and when they do find water, they can drink up to 40 gallons in one go, talk about rehydrating in style!

Touching a Baby Bird Will Make Its Mother Reject It

Myth: Baby birds come with a "do not touch" sticker.

Reality: Picture this: a baby bird has fallen from the nest, and you're there, thinking it's your moment to be a feathered hero. But then you remember the age-old warning: if you touch it, its mother will treat it like it's returned home after a year at college, with complete disinterest. Well, fear not! Most birds aren't equipped with a high-powered sniffer. Their sense of smell is relatively weak, so they are generally not going to notice a little eau de human on their chick. Here's the real tweet: Birds are pretty dedicated parents. The idea that they would abandon their offspring just because of a human scent is mostly a myth. They're more concerned with threats like predators or the loss of habitat. However, the reason wildlife experts preach hands-off is simple: even though momma bird might not snub junior, human interaction can lead to stress, injury, or unintentional removal from their natural environment.

So, while you're not turning the bird into an orphan by picking it up, you might still cause a flap. It's best to let nature tweet its own tune, and if you're really concerned, call in the wildlife pros who can handle the situation with care, feather gloves and all!

Frogs Will Stay in Water As It Slowly Heats to Boiling

Myth: Frogs can't handle their spa day turning into a hot pot.

Reality: Frogs might not have a degree in thermodynamics, but they're definitely not going to lounge around for a slow boil. This myth, often used as a metaphor for failing to notice gradual danger, doesn't hold water when it comes to actual amphibian behaviour. Frogs are ectothermic (cold-blooded), which means they rely on their environment to regulate their body temperature. If the water temperature starts to rise, they become uncomfortable long before the situation reaches a culinary climax. Their natural instinct to seek a stable, cool environment kicks in, prompting them to make a leap of faith out of warming waters. So, no, they're not sitting there contemplating their imminent transformation into frog stew, they're more likely planning their great escape to cooler, more comfortable waters. Their survival instinct is about as sharp as a French chef's knife, and they are not about to stick around for the main course!

Elephants Are Afraid of Mice

Myth: The mighty elephant, towering colossus of the savanna, lives in fear of the tiny, squeaky mouse.

Reality: Think of an elephant reacting to a mouse as you would to popcorn popping unexpectedly at night, not so much scared, just surprised! The myth that elephants are terrified of mice is more about cartoon physics than real-world animal behaviour. In reality, while elephants might be startled by the sudden movements or noises caused by a scurrying mouse, there's no evidence to suggest a deep-seated fear specific to these little critters. Elephants, with their impressively large ears, are highly sensitive to sound. They can detect both low-frequency rumbles and higher-pitched noises, which makes them keenly aware of any rustling in the grass that could indicate danger. This sensitivity is likely what sparks their alert responses, not so much a phobia of the mouse itself, but a general caution about unexpected small disturbances in their vicinity. This reaction is similar to how you might jump if a toaster suddenly pops while you're deep in thought. It's not that you're afraid of bread; it's just startling!

Sharks Don't Get Cancer

Myth: Sharks are the cancer-proof kings of the ocean.

Reality: Sharks might look tough with their sharp teeth and "I haven't slept in 400 million years" eyes, but they are not immune to cancer. This myth likely swam into popular belief because researchers observed that sharks seemed less susceptible to diseases, including cancer, compared to other species. However, studies and documented cases show that sharks can and do indeed get cancer. For instance, tumors have been found in Great White Sharks, Hammerheads, and even in the less fearsome species. The confusion might stem from sharks' impressive ability to heal quickly and their unique, somewhat more resistant immune system, which makes them fascinating subjects for medical research. Scientists are eager to unlock whether components of shark immune systems could help inspire new human cancer treatments. However, don't be fooled; these oceanic gladiators are not swimming around with a magical anti-cancer shield. They're just like any other animal in the kingdom, doing their best to stay healthy in a sea of potential problems. So, while sharks can't sign up for a cancer-free guarantee, they do keep scientists hooked with their biological mysteries!

A Cat's Purring Always Means It's Happy

Myth: A purring cat is a content cat, just chilling in its zen mode.

Reality: Think of a cat's purr as the Swiss Army knife of kitty communication, it's multi-functional! While we often interpret purring as a sign of happiness (and very often, it is), cats also use this trademark hum for a variety of other reasons. Purring can indeed signal contentment, but cats might also purr when they're feeling anything but chill. They can purr to express nervousness, fear, or even pain. Here's the fun part: Purring involves the rapid movement of the muscles of the larynx, combined with movement of the diaphragm. The sound is produced during both inhalation and exhalation, like a smooth, running engine. This isn't just any old body function, it's believed to be a form of self-healing. The frequency of a cat's purr, between 25 and 150 Hertz, happens to be in a range that promotes tissue regeneration. That's right, cats might actually be purring themselves better. It's as if they have a built-in biofeedback therapy session every time they decide to strike up the band!

Technology Myths

More Megapixels Mean Better Photos

Myth: Strap on a million megapixels, and you're the reincarnation of Ansel Adams.

Reality: If only photographic excellence were a simple game of megapixel Monopoly! While it's tempting to think that more megapixels guarantee superior images, this isn't exactly a pixel-perfect truth. Yes, a higher megapixel count means your camera can capture more detail, which is great if you plan to print your photos on billboards or crop them like a mad stylist. But here's the catch, more megapixels don't automatically translate to better photos. The real MVPs in capturing that drool-worthy shot are factors like sensor size, lens quality, and image processing. Think of it like this: if megapixels are the number of paint colors you have, the sensor size is the size of your canvas. A bigger sensor can capture more light, giving you better detail and reduced noise, especially in those moody low-light shots. It's like having a larger bucket to collect rain in a storm, the bigger the bucket, the more rain you catch. Then there's the lens quality, which could be likened to the quality of your paintbrush. A high-quality lens can make a huge difference in how sharp and vibrant your photos are, no matter how many pixels are packed into the sensor. It's all about how clearly you can paint the picture. Lastly, image processing is akin to your technique in turning those raw materials into a masterpiece. It's how the camera's brain interprets and enhances the raw data from the sensor to produce an image. Good image processing can correct flaws, manage colors, and balance shadows and highlights beautifully. So, the next time you're eyeing that 100-megapixel camera thinking it'll shoot you straight to photography stardom, remember, it's not just about how many pixels you pack. It's about how you use them. Without a good sensor, lens, and processor, your million-megapixel snapshot of a pizza might still end up looking like a mysterious UFO sighting rather than culinary art.

Macs Can't Get Viruses

Myth: Macs are like digital Fort Knox.

Reality: While Mac users might like to think their system is the digital equivalent of a superhero, immune to the mere mortal afflictions that plague PCs, the truth is a bit less glamorous. Yes, Macs can get viruses and other forms of malware. Initially, their Unix-based operating system does offer some robust security features which naturally make it a tough nut to crack. But let's not forget, malware authors love a challenge as much as the next coder.

The real kicker? As Macs have grown in popularity, they've become juicier targets. Hackers are like any of us, where the crowds go, they follow. And as they follow, they get craftier. Mac-specific threats have been on the rise, proving that malware is an equal opportunity annoyer, not discriminating by operating system. The myth probably persists because macOS does indeed include some strong security features that help protect against malware, such as Gatekeeper, which blocks unapproved software from running on your Mac without your agreement. However, no system is perfect. If a user is tricked into overriding these protection (think downloading and opening that "Totally_Not_a_Virus.dmg" file), their Mac can become infected just like a PC. So, while your Mac might have a decent security game, it's not invincible. Think of it more like a fortress with great walls, but if the gates are left open (or you invite the Trojan horse in for tea), trouble can still waltz right in.

Incognito Mode Means You Are Invisible Online

Myth: Incognito mode is like Harry Potter's invisibility cloak for browsing.

Reality: The truth is, incognito mode might better be compared to wearing sunglasses indoors, not quite invisible, just a little shady. When you switch to incognito or private browsing mode, your browser stops storing your search history, cookies, site data, and information entered in forms. This means that anyone else who uses your device won't see your activities. Handy, right? But here's the kicker: while incognito mode keeps your browsing history a secret from other users on the same device, it does little to shield you from the all-seeing eyes of the internet. Your internet service provider (ISP), for instance, can still track every site you visit, making you about as "invisible" as a lighthouse on a dark night. Similarly, if you're logged into your workplace or school network, the network administrators can keep tabs on your online antics.

And let's not forget the websites themselves! When you visit a site, the site's servers know you're there, even if you're in incognito mode. They might not know exactly who you are if you haven't logged in, but they know someone is visiting. Plus, if you log into a website while in incognito mode, that website knows exactly who you are and can track your activities on the site just like it normally would. So, think of incognito mode as a magic trick that only works in the room you're in. Outside that room? The magic's gone, and your activities are pretty much an open book. It's great for keeping gifts a surprise or hiding your embarrassing queries, but for true online privacy, you'll need more powerful spells like VPNs and secure browsers.

Leaving Your Phone Plugged in Overnight Kills the Battery

Myth: Charging overnight turns your smartphone battery into a pumpkin.

Reality: Fear not, midnight chargers! Modern smartphones are as clever as your grandma's secret cookie recipe. These smart devices are equipped with battery management systems that know when to stop charging. It's like they have an internal curfew, they stop the juice flow when the battery hits 100%, then let it sip power only occasionally to stay fully charged. Here's the scoop: Lithium-ion batteries, which power your beloved device, are designed to handle being plugged in. When you charge overnight, the phone will charge rapidly to 100%, then switch to a trickle charge, keeping your battery topped off without overloading it. This is like your phone taking tiny sips of coffee throughout the night instead of downing a double espresso shot. While this practice doesn't spell doom for your battery, unplugging once it's fully charged is still a good habit. It's a bit like turning off the tap while brushing your teeth, t saves resources. And let's face it, who doesn't want to feel just a bit more eco-friendly, even if we're really just concerned with keeping that battery bar green? So, go ahead, charge your phone by night without fear of it turning into a pumpkin by morning. Your smartphone's got your back, and you'll wake up to a fully charged device ready to tackle the day's digital demands, no fairy godmother required!

Private Browsing Protects You From Hackers

Myth: Private browsing is like a digital superhero defending you from evil hackers.

Reality: Unfortunately, private browsing is less of a superhero and more like a librarian who promises not to remember what books you checked out. Here's how it works: private browsing prevents your browser from saving your history, cookies, form data, and other information locally on your device. So, when you close that incognito window, it's as if your session never existed, at least to anyone who checks your device afterward. But let's burst this bubble: private browsing doesn't make you invisible to the rest of the internet. Your ISP (Internet Service Provider) can still see which websites you visit. The websites you visit can still collect data about you. And most importantly, hackers are still out there, sharpening their virtual knives, unaffected by your incognito mode. Think of it this way: if you're browsing the web on a Wi-Fi net-work that isn't secure (like that sketchy coffee shop Wi-Fi named "Free WiFi – No Hackers Here"), private browsing won't save you. Hackers can still intercept the data you send and receive, because private browsing doesn't encrypt your traffic. It's like walking through a glass maze thinking you're invisible because you can't see your reflection, meanwhile, everyone else can see you just fine. So, while private browsing can be handy for avoiding awkward conversations about why you were Googling "can cats eat spaghetti," it won't fend off cyber threats. For true online protection, you need a robust security setup: strong passwords, two-factor authentication, and maybe a trusty VPN. Otherwise, you're just a regular Joe with a browser wearing a very flimsy mask.

More Bars on Your Phone Means Better Service

Myth: Four bars = Blissful digital paradise..

Reality: Ah, the seductive lure of four bars on your phone, promising you a seamless Netflix binge or an uninterrupted group chat gossip session. But alas, reality is a fickle friend. Those bars merely indicate the signal strength to your nearest cell tower, not the actual quality of service you'll experience. Imagine those bars as a measure of how loudly you can shout *"HELLO!"* at the cell tower. You might be shouting loud and clear, but if everyone else is also shouting their own *"HELLO!"*, well, it turns into a cacophonous mess where no one gets through smoothly. Picture this: you're at a rock concert with a group of friends. You can see the stage perfectly (full bars), but so can thousands of other people. When everyone starts screaming their requests for the same song, the band's ability to hear any single voice diminishes (network congestion). Similarly, even with full bars, if too many users are trying to access the network at once, your data speeds can slow to a snail's pace. It's like trying to swim in a crowded pool, no matter how clear the water (signal strength), too many people make it hard to move (network quality). So, next time you see full bars and still struggle to load that cute cat video, remember: it's not about how loudly your phone can shout, but how many other phones are trying to shout at the same time

You Shouldn't Charge Your Phone Until It's Completely Dead

Myth: Phone batteries have the memory of an elephant.

Reality: Imagine your phone battery as a drama queen that loves a bit of attention. Lithium-ion batteries, which power most of our gadgets, actually prefer not to hit rock bottom before getting some juice. Unlike the old-school nickel-cadmium batteries that did have a "memory effect" (making them remember and grumble about partial charges), lithium-ion batteries thrive on little and often. Here's the scoop: These modern batteries have no memory, so they don't need to be completely drained before charging. In fact, keeping your battery level between 20% and 80% is the sweet spot. It's like keeping your snack levels topped up rather than waiting until you're hangry to eat. Lithium-ion batteries function by moving ions from the anode to the cathode through an electrolyte. If you constantly let the battery drain to 0%, it puts more strain on the battery and its chemical components. Imagine running your car on empty all the time, eventually, something's going to give, and it's not going to be pretty. Charging it before it's totally drained helps keep those ions happily flowing and extends the overall lifespan of the battery. So, think of your battery as a plant: give it regular sips of water (or charge) rather than letting it dry out completely and then drowning it. Your phone will thank you for these small, frequent top-ups with a longer life and better performance. No need for heroic zero-to-hero charging cycles here, just keep those ions moving and grooving!

Using a Cell Phone at a Gas Station Can Cause an Explosion

Myth: Your call could go out with a bang, turning your quick gas stop into a Michael Bay movie scene.

Reality: While the idea of cell phones igniting gas fumes makes for a thrilling Hollywood plot, it's more fiction than fact. This myth arises from theoretical concerns that the electromagnetic radiation from cell phones could ignite gasoline fumes. But let's be real: if this were true, our roads would be lined with smoldering craters instead of gas stations. Here's how it works: Cell phones emit a small amount of electromagnetic radiation, which isn't powerful enough to spark a fire. The chances of your phone triggering an explosion are about as high as you winning the lottery while being struck by lightning and bitten by a shark, all at the same time. In fact, the biggest culprits for gas station fires are static electricity and human clumsiness. Ever shuffled across the carpet in your socks and zapped yourself on a doorknob? Now imagine that tiny spark occurring while you're holding a gas nozzle. That's the real danger, not your phone's friendly chat with Aunt Marge. So next time you're at the pump, feel free to text, call, or check the latest cat memes. Just be sure to touch something metal to discharge any static before you reach for the nozzle. Your phone isn't going to blow up the gas station, but your wool sweater might give you a shocking surprise!

You Need to Defragment Your SSD

Myth: Treat your SSD like a hard drive; tidy up its room occasionally.

Reality: Imagine your SSD is a highly efficient librarian who can instantly find any book without having to walk around the library. Unlike traditional hard drives (HDDs) that rely on a spinning disk and a read/write head (like a frantic librarian running up and down aisles), SSDs store data on flash memory chips. This means they can access any piece of data just as quickly, no matter where it's located. Defragmentation is like reorganising all the books in a library to be in perfect order. This makes sense for HDDs because it reduces the time the librarian spends running around. But for our zen-like SSD librarian, all this unnecessary reorganisation just adds wear and tear. SSDs have a limited number of write cycles (like the librarian having a finite number of steps before needing a break). Defragmenting writes and rewrites a lot of data, which can actually shorten the lifespan of your SSD. So, don't bother with defragmenting, your SSD is a modern marvel that doesn't need to waste time on such trivial housekeeping. It's like trying to teach a robot how to alphabetise: impressive in theory, but totally unnecessary.

Closing Apps on Your Phone Saves Battery

Myth: Close your apps to keep your phone's battery from sprinting to zero.

Reality: This myth has convinced many a thumb to work overtime swiping apps away like an overzealous janitor. But here's the scoop: modern smartphones are pretty smart, they manage background apps better than you might think. When you close an app, it often stays in a "suspended" state, using minimal resources and battery. It's like putting the app to sleep rather than kicking it out of the house. When you reopen the app, your phone has to load it from scratch, which actually consumes more power than if you had just left it snoozing in the background. Think of it like this: constantly shutting down and restarting your apps is akin to opening and closing your fridge every time you want a snack instead of just grabbing everything at once. Your phone's operating system (iOS or Android) is built to juggle these sleeping apps efficiently, letting them nap without draining your battery.

So, unless an app is truly misbehaving, sucking down data, crashing, or eating more battery than Pac-Man munches dots, there's no need to play whack-a-mole with your recent apps screen. Let your phone handle the heavy lifting, and your battery will thank you with a little more juice at the end of the day.

Psychological Myths

Left-Brained People Are Logical, Right-Brained People Are Creative

Myth: Your brain's hemispheres are like a divided household

Reality: The idea that we're either left-brained logical robots or right-brained creative dreamers is as outdated as dial-up internet. While it's true that some functions are more dominant in one hemisphere than the other, our brains are all about teamwork. Imagine your brain as a rock band: the left hemisphere might be the drummer, keeping the beat with logic and order, while the right hemisphere plays lead guitar, shredding creative solos. But it's the whole band, he entire brain, that makes the music. Neuroscience has shown that tasks like reading, problem-solving, and even daydreaming light up networks across both hemispheres. For instance, language involves the left side for grammar and vocabulary, but the right side helps interpret context and tone. Creativity? That's a full-brain jam session where both sides contribute their unique talents. Studies using brain imaging reveal that our hemispheres constantly communicate through a bundle of nerves called the corpus callosum, ensuring both sides are in sync like the ultimate buddy cop duo. So, next time someone tells you they're "left-brained" and thus destined to a life of spreadsheets, or "right-brained" and therefore incapable of balancing a checkbook, remind them that their brain is an integrated masterpiece. Whether you're crunching numbers or creating art, your brain's hemispheres are working together like best friends on a road trip, each taking turns driving and navigating, ensuring you reach your destination with logic and creativity intact.

You Can Learn While You Sleep

Myth: Pop on some headphones and snooze your way to becoming fluent in Mandarin.

Reality: If only it were that simple! Imagine waking up one morning and suddenly speaking fluent Mandarin because you left a language tape playing overnight. Unfortunately, your brain isn't that cooperative. While sleep is crucial for memory consolidation, meaning it helps you process and store what you've learned during the day, it doesn't mean you can absorb new information through osmosis while you're in dreamland. Here's how it really works: During sleep, particularly the REM (Rapid Eye Movement) stage, your brain is busy sorting and filing away the day's experiences and learning. Think of it like a diligent librarian organising a mountain of new books. This process is vital for strengthening memories and making room for more knowledge. However, this librarian has a strict policy, no new book deliveries accepted during working hours! Trying to learn new information while you sleep is like asking the librarian to read and categorise books simultaneously while hosting a disco party.

Studies have shown that while your brain is a multitasking marvel, it draws the line at active learning during sleep. Those late-night Spanish podcasts might influence your dreams, but don't expect to wake up conjugating verbs flawlessly. If sleep-learning were real, universities would replace lecture halls with nap pods, and everyone would have PhDs by their senior year! So, while catching some Zs is fantastic for making sure today's hard work sticks, you'll need to stay awake to actually absorb and understand new material. Embrace your naps for what they are, a time for your brain to tidy up and refresh, because even the busiest librarian needs a break to keep things running smoothly.

You Only Have Five Senses

Myth: Your senses checklist stops at five

Reality: Humans actually have more than five senses, including balance (vestibular sense), temperature (thermoception), and pain (nociception). Your body is a sensory overachiever, so give it some credit! Let's take a closer look at your body's sensory superpowers:

Vestibular Sense: Picture this, you're walking a tightrope, and your vestibular sense is like that friend who holds your hand and keeps you from face-planting. Located in your inner ear, it helps you maintain balance and spatial orientation. Without it, you'd be falling over like a toddler after a sugar binge.

Thermoception: Ever wonder why you can tell when your coffee is just right without scalding your tongue? Thank your thermoception! It's your personal thermostat, scattered throughout your skin, making sure you know when things are hot, cold, or just right. Think of it as Goldilocks' guide to temperature.

Nociception: No, it's not an evil spell from Harry Potter. Nociception is your ability to sense pain. It's that hero that kicks in when you touch a hot stove or stub your toe, screaming *"Abort mission!"* and prompting you to pull away before you cause serious damage. Without it, you might end up with more burns and bruises than a clumsy circus performer.

Proprioception: Ever wonder how you can touch your nose with your eyes closed (assuming you haven't had a few too many drinks)? That's proprioception in action. It's your body's way of knowing where all your bits and pieces are without needing to look. It's like having a built-in GPS that helps you navigate your own limbs.

Interoception: This lesser-known sense keeps tabs on your internal state, like hunger, thirst, and the need to visit the bathroom. It's the reason you know when you're hungry before you turn into a hangry monster or why you start searching for a restroom after too much coffee.

Your sensory system is like a Swiss Army knife, equipped with all sorts of nifty tools to navigate the world.
 So next time you marvel at your five senses, remember there's a whole sensory orchestra playing behind the scenes, keeping you balanced, safe, and in tune with your environment.

Opposites Attract

Myth: A neat freak and a slob are destined for romance because they balance each other out.

Reality: While the idea of opposites attracting might make for a cute rom-com plot, in real life, it's more like mixing oil and water. Sure, opposites can be intriguing initially, after all, who doesn't enjoy a bit of variety? The slob might admire the neat freak's organisation, while the neat freak finds the slob's carefree attitude refreshing. It's like pairing a Type-A planner with a spontaneous adventure-seeker, sounds exciting, right? But here's the catch: when the honeymoon phase ends, the neat freak's love for tidy countertops clashes with the slob's creative interpretation of floordrobe" (you know, the wardrobe on the floor). The initial charm of being different can quickly turn into a daily grind of eye-rolling and "Why can't you just put the dishes in the dishwasher?" Studies have shown that long-term relationship satisfaction is often rooted in shared values and similarities, not dramatic differences. Couples who see eye-to-eye on key issues like cleanliness, finances, and lifestyle choices tend to have smoother sailing. It's less about *"You complete me"* and more about "We're on the same page." So, if you and your partner both geek out over color-coded planners, or if you both embrace the art of organised chaos, you're more likely to build a lasting connection. It's not that opposites can't make it work, but a shared love for clean countertops might just be the secret sauce to marital bliss. After all, who wants to argue over dirty socks when you can bond over the joy of a sparkling kitchen sink?

IQ Is Fixed and Determines Success

Myth: Your IQ is like your height, unchangeable

Reality: Imagine if life were that simple! You get one IQ score and your destiny is set in stone: "Sorry, you got a 98, so you'll be rocking a career in... rocks." Fortunately, reality is far more flexible and forgiving. Here's the scoop: IQ, or Intelligence Quotient, is a measure of certain cognitive abilities. While your IQ score can give a snapshot of certain mental skills at a specific point in time, it's not a static number etched into your brain with a laser. Studies show that IQ can actually change throughout your life. Just like muscles, your brain can get stronger with the right exercise, learning new skills, solving puzzles, engaging in stimulating conversations (yes, even those intense debates about which superhero is the best). But wait, there's more! Success isn't just about how well you can solve logic puzzles or remember obscure facts about the Roman Empire. Emotional intelligence (EQ), the ability to understand and manage your own emotions and those of others, plays a huge role. Think of EQ as your social superpower. A high EQ helps you navigate the social jungle, build strong relationships, and handle life's curveballs with the grace of a cat on a Roomba. And then there's good old perseverance. Ever heard the story of the tortoise and the hare? It's not always the smartest (or fastest) who wins, but the one who keeps chugging along despite setbacks. Grit, determination, and a refusal to give up when things get tough are often the secret sauce behind many success stories. So, if you hit a mental roadblock, channel your inner tortoise and keep on moving. Lastly, social skills are the unsung heroes of success. You could be a genius, but if you can't communicate your ideas, negotiate, or collaborate with others, you might find yourself stuck in the lab alone while your socially adept colleagues are out there conquering the world. Think of it this way: even the most brilliant invention needs a good pitch to make it big. So, instead of worrying about whether your IQ is high enough to unlock the gates of success, focus on developing a well-rounded skill set. Play the game with all the cards in your deck, intelligence, emotional savvy, perseverance, and social finesse. It's not about the hand you're dealt, but how you play it that counts. And who knows, with the right strategy, you might just find yourself collecting accolades instead of rocks.

Mental Illness Is Rare

Myth: Mental illness is like finding a four-leaf clover

Reality: Actually, mental illness is as common as a dandelion in your lawn. You know, those yellow flowers you pretend are weeds but secretly kind of admire for their resilience? About 1 in 5 adults experience some form of mental illness each year. That's like saying if you invited five friends over for dinner, one of them might need to have a heart-to-heart about their mental health. How It Works: Mental illness can take many forms, depression, anxiety, bipolar disorder, and more. It's not like a unicorn sighting; it's more like that persistent dandelion showing up in your yard every spring. It doesn't mean your lawn is doomed, just that it needs some attention. Mental health issues arise from a complex mix of genetics, environment, and life experiences. It's like a soup with too many ingredients, sometimes it turns out great, sometimes it needs a bit of tweaking. People often hide their struggles because of stigma, but let's be honest, ignoring mental health is as effective as ignoring that dandelion. Just like those resilient little flowers, mental health issues won't just disappear if you pretend they're not there. They need understanding, care, and sometimes professional help to manage.

All Therapy Involves Lying on a Couch Talking About Your Childhood

Myth: Therapy means endless sessions of *"Tell me about your mother"*.

Reality: Let's burst this couch-and-childhood bubble! Modern therapy is as diverse as a box of chocolates, you never know what you're going to get, but it's tailored just for you. Not every therapist is channeling Freud, and your therapy sessions might involve anything from cognitive behavioral techniques to mindfulness exercises. Imagine therapy like a workout for your brain, sometimes it's yoga, stretching out those mental knots; other times, it's a high-intensity interval session, tackling issues head-on with rapid-fire strategies. Therapists are like personal trainers, but for your mind. They might ask about your past if it's tripping up your present, but they're just as likely to help you plot a course for future triumphs.

There's Cognitive Behavioural Therapy (CBT), which is like having a mental fitness coach who helps you challenge negative thoughts and swap them for positive ones, no couch required. Or you might try Eye Movement Desensitization and Reprocessing

(EMDR), which sounds sci-fi but involves moving your eyes in specific ways to process traumatic memories, more like a dance party for your eyes than a snooze on a sofa. And let's not forget group therapy, where you don't lie on a couch but might sit in a circle, share your thoughts, and realize you're not alone in your experiences. It's like a support group with a therapist as the MC, keeping things constructive and insightful. So, next time someone mentions therapy, think of a dynamic, supportive environment where you're actively engaged in exercises that can range from talking through your issues to practicing new skills. Therapy is about working with what's happening now and steering towards a better future, with a skilled navigator by your side, and, most importantly, no compulsory couch!

Antidepressants Make You Happy All the Time

Myth: Pop an antidepressant, and you'll be riding a constant high like a human balloon.

Reality: Picture this: you take an antidepressant and suddenly you're grinning like the Cheshire Cat, handing out high-fives to strangers, and seeing rainbows everywhere. Not quite. Antidepressants aren't magical happy pills; they're more like brain balance assistants. These meds help adjust the levels of neurotransmitters, think serotonin and norepinephrine, so your brain's mood orchestra plays a more harmonious tune instead of a chaotic free jazz session. Imagine your brain is a big, complicated office. Depression can make it feel like everyone's either missing or just throwing papers in the air. Antidepressants come in, not as the office party planners, but as the meticulous organizers, ensuring that everyone gets back to their desks and does their jobs properly. This doesn't mean the office is now a carnival; it's just functioning normally again.

So, if you're expecting to float on cloud nine with confetti cannons going off, you might be in for a surprise. Antidepressants are there to help you navigate back to a state of emotional stability, where you can experience the full range of human emotions.

Weather Myths

Lightning Never Strikes the Same Place Twice

Myth: Lightning has a strict one-strike policy.

Reality: Lightning doesn't keep score! It can and often does strike the same place multiple times, especially tall, pointy objects like skyscrapers or trees. The Empire State Building, for instance, gets zapped about 20-25 times a year. It's like lightning's favorite hangout spot, VIP access only! Here's how it works: Lightning forms when there's a buildup of electrical charges in storm clouds. These clouds act like giant batteries, with the top part being positively charged and the bottom part negatively charged. The ground underneath the storm gets positively charged in response, setting the stage for a shocking performance. When the electrical potential between the cloud and the ground gets high enough, BAM! A lightning bolt forms. The bolt seeks out the path of least resistance, often finding the tallest, pointiest objects to connect with, like a moth to a flame. It doesn't care if it's struck there before, tall and pointy is always in fashion.

Now, imagine the Empire State Building, standing tall and proud in New York City. It's practically waving at the storm clouds, saying, *"Pick me, pick me!"* With its impressive height of

1,454 feet, it offers an easy path for the electrical charges to meet. So, it's no wonder lightning keeps coming back for more, like a loyal customer at its favorite diner. In fact, lightning loves some places so much that they've become legends in the lightning world. Take the Tampa Bay area in Florida, dubbed the "Lightning Capital of North America." Storms roll through there with such frequency that locals could probably set their watches by the strikes. So, next time you hear someone say lightning never strikes the same place twice, just smile and think of the Empire State Building, getting its regular 20-25 high-voltage kisses a year. Lightning's not picky, it's just looking for the fastest route to the ground and a repeat customer is always welcome.

Tornadoes Always Move in the Same Direction

Myth: Tornadoes are creatures of habit

Reality: Tornadoes are like teenagers, they go wherever they want, whenever they want, and they're impossible to predict! Picture a tornado as a rebellious teen with a mind of its own. One minute it's heading north, then suddenly it's like, *"Nah, let's check out what's happening to the west,"* and makes a sharp turn. These whirling dervishes of destruction can change direction, speed up, slow down, or even make U-turns without a care in the world. Here's the scoop: Tornadoes form from supercell thunderstorms, which are highly organized and rotating storm systems. The path a tornado takes is influenced by the storm's internal dynamics and the larger-scale winds in the atmosphere. Think of it like this: the supercell is the tornado's wild chaperone, and wherever it goes, the tornado follows, albeit in a sometimes zigzagging, unpredictable manner. Just like you wouldn't trust a teenager with your car keys, you can't trust a tornado to stick to a predictable path. Meteorologists use radar and storm-spotting techniques to track these twisters, but even with all their gadgets, predicting the exact path of a tornado is like trying to guess the next move of a cat chasing a laser pointer. So, next time you hear there's a tornado warning, remember: these twisters are the ultimate free spirits of the weather world. They don't follow maps, and they certainly don't take requests. Stay safe, take cover, and let those unpredictable tornadoes have their wild, wandering ways!

Hot Water Freezes Faster than Cold Water

Myth: Boil your water for ice cubes in a hurry!

Reality: This myth, known as the Mpemba effect, is the black sheep of the physics family, constantly debated, occasionally believed, but never fully understood. The Mpemba effect suggests that hot water can sometimes freeze faster than cold water under specific conditions. It's like the rebel teenager of the scientific world, unpredictable and always causing a stir at family dinners. Here's a bit more on how it works (or doesn't): When you heat water, a few things happen that might give hot water a freezing head start. First, some of the hot water evaporates, reducing the overall volume that needs to freeze. It's like trimming the fat before a race. Second, hot water can create convection currents, mixing more uniformly as it cools down. This uniformity might help it lose heat faster. Lastly, dissolved gases in cold water can make it harder to freeze, and heating the water releases these gases. However, before you start boiling water for your next ice cube tray, know this: the Mpemba effect is as fickle as a cat deciding whether to sit on your lap. The exact conditions for this phenomenon to occur are still a mystery, with scientists scratching their heads and arguing about it at physics conferences. So, for your next cocktail party, stick to the tried-and-true method: cold water. Unless you're looking to conduct a mini-experiment in your freezer (complete with safety goggles and a lab coat for dramatic effect), it's best to leave the boiling water for your tea. You'll save yourself some time, and your guests won't have to wait an eternity for their drinks.

Clouds Are Weightless

Myth: Clouds are fluffy, weightless cotton candy in the sky

Reality: Think again! Those fluffy clouds are actually heavyweights, with an average cumulus cloud weighing in at around a million pounds. That's about the same as 100 elephants having a group hug in the sky! Here's how it works: A cloud forms when warm air rises, expands, and cools. As the air cools, it can't hold as much water vapor, which condenses into tiny water droplets or ice crystals. These droplets are so small that they remain suspended in the air, supported by the same rising warm air that brought them up there in the first place. Imagine trying to juggle a million-pound water balloon, pretty tricky, right? But the atmosphere is a skilled juggler, balancing all those droplets effortlessly. The secret lies in the size of the droplets; each one is minuscule, so the upward movement of warm air can keep them aloft. When enough of these droplets clump together, they form the fluffy, white clouds we see. So, next time you gaze up at those puffy wonders, remember they're more like secret sumo wrestlers in disguise. Give them some respect, they're not just floating on air; they're defying gravity with style!

Heat Lightning is Different from Regular Lightning

Myth: Heat lightning is a special, benign summer phenomenon.

Reality: Ah, the mysterious heat lightning, often seen on sultry summer nights, flashing silently on the horizon like nature's own disco lights. But guess what? Heat lightning is just regular lightning practicing social distancing. Here's the scoop: Lightning is essentially a giant spark of electricity in the atmosphere between clouds, the air, or the ground. When you see heat lightning, you're actually watching lightning from a thunderstorm so far away that the sound of the thunder can't reach your ears. Thunder only travels about 10 miles before it fades away, while lightning can be seen much further away, depending on the conditions. Think of it this way: it's like spotting a distant concert from your bedroom window. You can see the flashing lights of the stage, but you can't hear the music. It's not a quieter, gentler concert, it's just far enough away that the sound doesn't reach you.

So, why is it called "heat lightning"? Because these flashes are often spotted on warm, humid nights when distant thunderstorms are common. People once thought the heat itself was generating the lightning, but in reality, it's just your average, everyday storm doing its thing a few dozen miles away. No need to worry, though, this distant light show isn't any safer than the up-close-and-personal variety. Lightning, no matter how far, is still just as electrifying.

Cows Lie Down When It's About to Rain

Myth: Cows are the farmyard weather forecasters.

Reality: If cows were meteorologists, they'd have a pretty cushy job, mostly lying around, chewing cud, and occasionally moving to a more comfortable spot. The truth is, cows lie down for a variety of reasons that have nothing to do with rain. They might be tired, taking a break, or just finding a comfy spot to chew their cud in peace. The myth likely stems from observations that cows sometimes lie down before a storm, but correlation doesn't equal causation. Just because a cow plops down and it happens to rain later doesn't mean the cow had a premonition. It's like saying your cat's ability to knock things off the counter predicts earthquakes, entertaining, but not scientifically sound. Cows also lie down to regulate their body temperature. When it's hot, lying down can help them cool off by reducing the amount of their body exposed to the sun. Conversely, when it's cold or the ground is damp, they might stand to stay warmer and drier. So, if a cow is lying down, it's just doing its thing, not channeling its inner weather forecaster.

Hail Only Falls in the Summer

Myth: Hailstones are a summer-exclusive event.

Reality: Hailstones are equal-opportunity ice throwers and can make an appearance any time of the year if the conditions are right. Picture this: updrafts in a thunderstorm are like nature's elevators for raindrops. These updrafts swoop in and whisk the raindrops high up into the atmosphere, where it's colder than your ex's heart. Up there, the raindrops freeze into little ice pellets. But wait, there's more! These ice pellets can get caught in the storm's wild updraft party multiple times, collecting more layers of ice each trip, turning into bigger and bigger hailstones. Eventually, gravity gets tired of this charade and pulls them down, raining icy vengeance on everything below. So, while summer storms might get all the hail hype because they're more intense, don't be surprised if you find yourself in a spring or autumn hailstorm. Just remember to take cover and enjoy the icy spectacle from a safe distance, hailstones don't care about the calendar, they just want to crash the party whenever the storm conditions let them.

Snow is White

Myth: Snowflakes are pure, pristine white.
Reality: Hold onto your sleds! Snow is actually transparent. That's right, each tiny snowflake is as clear as a piece of glass. But before you start questioning your eyesight, here's the scoop: Snow appears white because of the way light scatters when it hits the complex structure of ice crystals. Think of snowflakes as nature's little disco balls. When sunlight (which is made up of all the colors of the rainbow) hits these intricate ice crystals, it bounces around and gets scattered in all directions. This scattering causes all the colors to mix together, and our eyes see the result as white. It's like the snowflakes are putting on a light show just for you! Under certain conditions, snow can even take on different hues. Ever noticed how snow can sometimes look blue in the shadows? That's because the light is scattered even more, making the blue wavelengths more noticeable. And if you've ever seen pink snow, it's not your imagination, it could be due to algae that thrive in cold conditions, turning the snow a lovely shade of watermelon. So, the next time you're admiring a snowy scene, remember: snow isn't showing off its wardrobe of pure white. It's just bending light in all the right ways, proving that even frozen water has a flair for drama and a knack for playing with the spectrum!

Survival Myths

You Can Suck Out Snake Venom

Myth: Channel your inner cowboy and suck that venom out!

Reality: Sooo... you're in the wilderness, your friend gets bitten by a snake, and suddenly you think you're in an old western. You roll up your sleeves, ready to play the hero by sucking out the venom. Not so fast, cowboy! Here's the lowdown: trying to suck out snake venom is about as effective as trying to un-toast a piece of bread. For starters, you're likely to end up with venom in your mouth, which is a terrible idea unless you're aiming for a sequel of "Snakebite Victim: The Double Feature." Plus, saliva isn't exactly sterile, so you might just add an infection to the mix, turning a bad day into a truly awful one. The proper way to handle a snakebite is to keep the victim calm (no cowboy yodeling, please), and immobilize the bite area to slow the spread of venom. Keep the affected limb at or below heart level if possible. Instead of playing doctor, get professional medical help as quickly as you can. Real-life snakebite kits? They're often just as useless as our Wild West antics. In reality, the best thing to suck on after a snakebite is a phone, so you can call for medical assistance pronto. Leave the snakebite heroics to the silver screen and focus on keeping your friend safe and sound until the professionals take over. Yeehaw!

Alexander C.

Moss Always Grows on the North Side of Trees

Myth: Lost in the woods? Just find some mossy trees to navigate!

Reality: Imagine trusting moss for navigation, it's like relying on a cat to lead you to the nearest fish market. Moss is an equal-opportunity grower, thriving wherever conditions are moist and shady. It could be north, south, east, or west. Here's the scoop: moss doesn't care about your compass. It's more interested in humidity and shade. Moss loves hanging out in damp, shady spots, and these can be found all around the tree, depending on the environment. So, why does this myth exist? In the northern hemisphere, the north side of trees tends to be shadier and damper, making it a cozy spot for moss. But it's not a hard-and-fast rule. Trees in dense forests, near rivers, or in shaded valleys can have moss on any side. Moss isn't exactly a team player in your navigation club, it's more like a fair-weather friend who shows up wherever conditions suit it best.

Rub Frostbitten Skin to Warm It Up

Myth: Feeling frosty? Just rub your hands together like you're starting a campfire!

Reality: Hold up there, Frosty the Snowman! Rubbing frostbitten skin can actually make things a whole lot worse. Imagine your tissues are like delicate little snowflakes. When you rub them, you're essentially breaking those snowflakes into icy shards that can cause even more damage. It's like taking a fragile ice sculpture and giving it a good whack with a sledgehammer, probably not the outcome you were hoping for. Here's the deal: Frostbite happens when your skin and the tissues beneath it freeze. The best way to treat it is to warm the affected area gently. Think of it as giving your skin a warm hug rather than a rough massage. Use lukewarm water (around 104-107°F or 40-42°C) to slowly thaw out the frostbitten area. This way, you're melting the ice crystals safely without turning your skin into a battlefield of broken ice daggers. Also, don't use hot water or direct heat sources like a fire or heating pad. Your frostbitten skin has lost its sense of temperature and might end up with burns, adding insult to injury. Stick to the gentle, lukewarm bath approach. Your skin will thank you, and you'll avoid looking like you just escaped from a medieval torture chamber. So, next time you're channeling your inner Arctic explorer and you feel the frostbite creeping in, remember: no rubbing! Opt for a gentle thaw instead of an enthusiastic scrub. Your future, frostbite-free self will give you a warm round of applause.

You Can Drink Your Own Pee in a Survival Situation

Myth: When thirsty, just recycle, pee is mostly water, right?

Reality: Drinking urine is like drinking salty soup, it's dehydrating. Urine contains waste products your body is trying to eliminate, not something you want to reintroduce. If you're stranded, focus on finding a real water source instead of turning into Bear Grylls. Sure, urine is mostly water, but it's also the body's liquid garbage truck, hauling away waste products like urea, salts, and other stuff you really don't want to drink. Imagine sipping on a cocktail made from yesterday's junk mail. Doesn't sound too appealing, does it? When you're dehydrated, your kidneys work hard to concentrate urine to conserve water, making it even saltier and less hydrating, think of it as nature's salty lemonade, but far less refreshing. Drinking it can further stress your kidneys, pushing them towards a meltdown worthy of a reality TV show. In extreme cases, like a dry, sun-baked desert, the myth might make you think, *"Hey, desperate times, right?"* But guzzling your own pee can accelerate dehydration, potentially leading to nausea and quicker exhaustion. Your body wanted that stuff out for a reason, forcing it back in is like re-watching the worst movie of your life on a loop. Instead, if you're lost in the wilderness, channel your inner explorer and focus on finding a real water source. Look for signs of water like animal tracks leading to a stream, dew on plants in the morning, or even solar stills if you have the know-how. You'll fare much better hydrating with these options rather than sipping your own brand of salty soup. Remember, Bear Grylls does it for TV ratings, you should aim for actual survival.

If You're Stabbed, Pull the Knife Out

Myth: Got a knife sticking out of you? Yank it out like you're in an action movie!

Reality: Whoa there, Rambo! Removing a knife from a stab wound can quickly turn you from action hero to horror movie victim. Here's why: When the knife is lodged in your body, it might be blocking a major blood vessel or keeping your insides from becoming outsides. Pulling it out is like removing a cork from a bottle of vintage *"Ouch, That Hurts!"* wine, suddenly, everything starts flowing, and not in a good way. Think of the knife as an uninvited guest at a party. Sure, you want it gone, but ripping it out unceremoniously will just cause chaos. Instead, let the professionals handle it. They have the skills, the tools, and the sterile environment to prevent your impromptu surgery from turning into a Quentin Tarantino bloodbath. So, resist the urge to play surgeon. Keep the knife where it is, stabilize it with some gauze or cloth (a clean shirt works if you're out of gauze), and get yourself to the nearest emergency room. Your job is to stay calm and avoid fainting like a Victorian damsel, not to audition for a real-life sword-in-the-stone moment. Let the medical experts remove the knife with the care and precision it takes to handle such a sticky situation. They'll make sure your story ends with a laugh, not a scream!

Alexander C.

Punch a Shark in the Nose to Escape an Attack

Myth: Channel your inner Rocky and sock that shark right in the snout!

Reality: Picture this: You're in the ocean, enjoying a leisurely swim, when suddenly, you see a shark. Your first thought might be, "Time to turn into a marine boxer and go for the nose!" But hold up, hitting a moving shark on its nose is about as easy as threading a needle while riding a rollercoaster. Here's the scoop: A shark's nose is indeed sensitive due to the ampullae of Lorenzini, tiny, jelly-filled pores that detect electric fields in the water. However, in the middle of a shark attack, aiming for this sensitive spot is like trying to poke a pinhole in a water balloon while it's flying towards your face. Not exactly a piece of cake. Instead, go for the shark's eyes or gills, which are much larger targets and equally sensitive. The eyes, being soft and unprotected, are the shark's visual windows to the world, and they don't take kindly to being poked. The gills are another vulnerable area, think of them as the shark's version of lungs. Interrupting their breathing process is a quick way to convince Mr. Jaws to back off. So, if you find yourself in this unfortunate underwater showdown, forget the Hollywood heroics. Focus on making your getaway by targeting the eyes or gills.

Playing Dead Will Save You from a Bear Attack

Myth: Bears respect the dead and will leave you alone if you play possum.

Reality: Hold your horses, or rather, your bears! Playing dead can sometimes be a good idea, but it's not a one-size-fits-all solution. Let's break it down by bear type so you don't end up getting a one-star review for your possum impersonation.

Grizzly Bears: If you encounter a grizzly and it's charging you, dropping to the ground and playing dead might actually work. Lie flat on your stomach, cover your neck with your hands, and spread your legs to make it harder for the bear to flip you over. Grizzlies are more likely to see you as a non-threat if you're playing possum. But be prepared for the bear to give you a curious nudge or two, it's not checking your pulse, just making sure you're really down for the count. Once the bear loses interest, stay still until you're sure it's gone. Remember, you're auditioning for a drama, not a slapstick comedy.

Black Bears: These guys are a different story. If you play dead in front of a black bear, you might as well put a "buffet" sign on your back. Black bears are more likely to see you as easy prey if you're lying there like a motionless meatloaf. Instead, stand your ground, make yourself look big, and make lots of noise. Think of it as a bear-appropriate karaoke session, sing loudly and off-key. Clap your hands, wave your arms, and show that bear you're not someone to be messed with. Knowing Your Bears: The trick is knowing which bear you're dealing with. Grizzlies have a hump on their shoulders and shorter, rounder ears, while black bears are smaller with no shoulder hump and longer, pointier ears. If you're unsure, just remember: grizzly, play dead (but not too convincingly), black bear, channel your inner rock star.

Running in a Zigzag Pattern Escapes Alligators

Myth: Outrun that gator by zigzagging like a football player!

Reality: Picture this: You're being chased by an alligator, and someone yells, "Zigzag!" So you start darting left and right like a confused squirrel. While this might entertain any onlookers (and the alligator), it's not the best survival strategy. Here's the scoop: Alligators can reach speeds of up to 11 mph in short bursts on land, but they're sprinters, not marathon runners. They get tired quickly, so your best bet is to run straight and fast, channeling your inner Usain Bolt. Zigzagging wastes precious time and energy, and you might end up tripping over your own feet or, worse, running right into the gator's hungry jaws. Imagine trying to dodge a gator like you're in a dance-off with the "Gatorade Shuffle." It's more likely to leave you with a twisted ankle than a ticket to safety. Instead, make a beeline for the nearest tree, car, or sturdy structure. And remember, alligators are built for swimming, not land pursuits, once you've put some distance between you and the gator, you're likely in the clear.

Cacti Are a Reliable Water Source

Myth: Stuck in the desert? Just crack open a cactus for a refreshing drink!

Reality: Ah, the trusty cactus, nature's supposed water cooler in the desert. But wait! Before you go whacking that prickly plant open like it's a piñata full of Gatorade, let's set the record straight. Most cacti are filled with a bitter, slimy goo that's about as refreshing as a mouthful of expired milk. This goo contains alkaloids and other chemicals that can upset your stomach, making you more dehydrated due to vomiting or diarrhea. Imagine being stranded in the desert and having a "Who drank the bad cactus water?" moment. Not pretty. So, how does it work? Cacti have adapted to store water, but this water is mixed with substances that help them survive the harsh conditions, not quench your thirst. Their internal moisture is more like a protective slime, deterring animals (and desperate humans) from indulging. If you find yourself wandering the desert, parched and contemplating a cactus snack, it's better to look for more reliable cactus signs of water. Damp ground, green vegetation, or following the tracks of animals (who tend to know where to find a drink) are your best bets. Basically, trust the desert critters, hey've been to survival school, and they didn't flunk out like some myths! So, unless you want your desert adventure to include a cameo by Montezuma's Revenge, steer clear of the cactus cocktail. Nature's water coolers come with some serious strings attached, and your stomach will thank you for passing them by.

Parenting Myths

Picking Up a Crying Baby Spoils Them

Myth: If you pick up your crying baby, they'll turn into a spoiled brat.

Reality: Babies cry because it's their only way to communicate. Think of it as their version of texting you, *"Hey, I need something!"* Ignoring those cries doesn't teach them independence; it teaches them that their parents are mysteriously deaf. When you respond to their cries, you're not spoiling them. You're helping them feel secure and building trust, which is crucial for their emotional development. Imagine if you texted your best friend about an emergency, and they just ghosted you. That's how your baby feels when their cries go unanswered. By picking them up, you're basically saying, *"I've got your back, little one."* This reassurance helps them develop a sense of safety, and they grow up feeling confident that the world is a good place, thanks to you! Spoiling them? Not quite. Instead, you're raising a future world leader who knows how to express themselves. Today's cry for a diaper change could very well translate into tomorrow's keynote speech at the UN. So, the next time someone tells you that picking up your baby will spoil them, just smile and say, *"I'm not raising a tyrant, I'm nurturing a diplomat!"*

You Have to Childproof Everything or Disaster Will Strike

Myth: Your house must resemble a padded cell or your child will be in constant peril.

Reality: While it's smart to make your home safe, you don't need to transform it into Fort Knox. Here's why: Childproofing should focus on major hazards, think sharp corners, toxic substances, and heavy objects that can topple over, not encasing your furniture in foam. Safety gates, cabinet locks, and socket covers are helpful, but you don't need to bubble-wrap your entire living room. Instead of creating a house-sized hamster ball, balance childproofing with supervision and teaching. Picture this: your toddler takes their first wobbly steps and inevitably tumbles. You rush over, comfort them, and voila, they've learned something valuable about gravity and balance. Plus, a little bump here and there is part of growing up. It teaches resilience and that gravity is not just a good idea; it's the law!

Your house is a learning environment, not a minefield. Kids are natural explorers, and while they'll inevitably face some minor bumps and bruises, these experiences help them understand their limits and develop coordination. Besides, if you covered every surface with foam, they'd miss out on learning how to navigate the real world, where not everything is as soft as their favorite teddy bear. So, relax and remember: a few well-placed safety measures combined with active supervision and teaching your child about safety will do the trick. Plus, who wants to live in a house that looks like a packing material factory? Not you, and certainly not your little explorer.

TV Turns Kids into Zombies

Myth: One episode of cartoons and your kid's brain will turn to mush.

Reality: Hold onto your remote control, because this myth is about as real as Bigfoot riding a unicorn! The key here is moderation. Letting your kids watch TV doesn't mean they're destined for a future as mindless couch potatoes. In fact, educational programs can be superheroes for young minds, teaching them everything from letters and numbers to social skills and empathy. Take Sesame Street, for example. This beloved show has been nurturing young brains since the days when bell-bottoms were in fashion. It's packed with lessons on diversity, kindness, and problem-solving, all delivered by a friendly cast of furry monsters and a giant bird who seems suspiciously knowledgeable for someone who lives in a nest. Kermit the Frog might even pop in with a life lesson or two, his TED Talks are truly riveting. Research shows that kids can learn a lot from well-designed TV shows. According to the American Academy of Pediatrics, educational TV can improve cognitive skills and enhance learning when used appropriately. It's like having a classroom in your living room, minus the need for permission slips and parent-teacher conferences. Plus, a bit of screen time gives you a chance to sneak in some much-needed downtime. Imagine this: Your child is happily engaged with a show about counting to ten with a dancing elephant, and you get a few precious moments to sip your coffee while it's still hot. It's a win-win situation! So, the next time someone warns you about TV turning your child into a brainless zombie, you can confidently tell them that as long as it's balanced with other activities, like playing outside, reading books, and building epic pillow forts, TV can be a valuable part of a well-rounded childhood. And if anyone doubts you, just point to Sesame Street's impressive track record. If it's good enough for generations of happy, healthy kids, it's good enough for yours!

Good Parents Never Get Angry

Myth: Great parents are like Zen monks, never raising their voice.

Reality: Even Zen monks have days where they'd rather throw their meditation cushions out the window. Parenting is tough, and feeling angry sometimes is as natural as toddlers rejecting vegetables. Here's the scoop: anger is a normal emotion, and everyone experiences it, even parents who seem like they have it all together. The key isn't to never get angry (because, let's be real, that's impossible), but to handle it in a way that sets a good example. Imagine your child sees you feeling frustrated because the dog just chewed up their homework(again). Instead of transforming into the Hulk, you take a deep breath, maybe even mutter a calming mantra, and explain, "I'm really upset right now, but I need to take a moment to calm down." By doing this, you're showing your mini-me how to deal with strong emotions constructively. It's like giving them an emotional toolkit: "See, when life hands you a chewed-up mess, you don't have to lose it. You can stay cool and handle it like a pro." They learn that it's okay to feel anger, but it's even better to manage it without causing a scene worthy of reality TV. So, no need to beat yourself up if you feel angry. The goal isn't perfection; it's progress. Every time you model calmness and control, even after a slip-up, you're teaching resilience and emotional intelligence. Remember, even the Dalai Lama probably gets annoyed when he stubs his toe, what counts is how you bounce back and move forward. That's gold-star parenting, right there, and your kiddo is taking notes, even if it looks like they're just doodling on the walls.

If Your Child Misbehaves, You're a Bad Parent

Myth: Your child throws a tantrum in the store, and everyone thinks you're raising a future supervillain.

Reality: Imagine this: you're cruising through the supermarket, your cart is full of groceries, and suddenly your adorable angel transforms into a banshee because you said no to the fifth pack of gummy bears. You feel the eyes of every shopper bore into your soul, judging you as if you just announced a plan to take over the world. But listen, kids are tiny humans learning to navigate big emotions and the complicated world around them. Their tantrums are more about their developing brains struggling to cope with disappointment than your parenting skills. Picture it as their internal WiFi signal dropping out, they're buffering, not broken. Experts agree that occasional meltdowns are as normal as that one sock mysteriously going missing in the laundry. The trick is consistent, loving guidance. This means calmly setting boundaries, offering comfort, and teaching them how to manage their feelings. It's a bit like being an emotional traffic cop, directing them towards calm, one meltdown at a time. So, next time your kid decides to perform their rendition of "The Floor is Lava" in aisle 5, remember: this is not an audition for "Parents

Gone Wild." It's a normal part of their growth. Consistency, patience, and love will guide them through, and you'll get through the stares from the peanut gallery with your head held high. Because if parenting were easy, it wouldn't come with such fantastic stories to laugh about later!

Parents Must Entertain Their Kids 24/7

Myth: If you're not playing with your kids every moment, you're failing.

Reality: Contrary to popular belief, your child doesn't need you to be their personal cruise director at all times. Independent play is like a superfood for their developing brains. It fosters creativity, problem-solving skills, and resilience. When kids play on their own, they learn to entertain themselves, imagine new worlds, and solve conflicts without a referee. Picture this: your child decides to build a pillow fort. As they arrange cushions and drape blankets, they're not just making a mess, they're engineering a masterpiece. They're planning, experimenting, and maybe even negotiating with a sibling over the prime pillow real estate. These activities are crucial for developing cognitive and social skills. Meanwhile, you, dear parent, get a chance to sit down. Imagine sipping a cup of coffee that's actually hot. Maybe you even get to read a book, scroll through your phone, or just stare into space and remember what quiet sounds like. This break isn't just good for your sanity, it models for your kids that adults need time to relax and recharge too. So, let's bust this myth wide open: you don't have to be a 24/7 entertainer. Your kids need their space to grow, and you need your space to breathe. The next time your child says they're bored, smile and say, "That's the sound of your imagination warming up." Then, watch as they dive into a world of their own making. Everyone wins: your child becomes more self-sufficient, and you reclaim a slice of peace. It's parenting magic.

Perfect Parents Exist

Myth: Somewhere, there's a parent who never makes a mistake.

Reality: Perfect parents are as real as unicorns riding on rainbows. Spoiler alert: They don't exist. Parenting is more like trying to juggle flaming torches while riding a unicycle, blindfolded. Everyone stumbles, and that's okay! Those mistakes and imperfections are part of the gig. When you accidentally send your kid to school with mismatched socks or forget to pack their lunch, you're actually teaching them valuable life lessons. Think about it: If kids only saw perfection, they'd grow up with unrealistic expectations and a fear of failure. Your glorious missteps show them that it's okay to make mistakes and learn from them. It builds resilience and emphasizes the importance of effort and perseverance over flawlessness. After all, life isn't a perfectly curated Instagram feed; it's more like a blooper reel with heartfelt moments. So, the next time you burn dinner or send your kid to school dressed as a pirate on the wrong day, remember: you're not failing; you're parenting! Celebrate the chaos, laugh at the mishaps, and know that you're doing your best. And if anyone tells you they've got it all figured out, ask them to show you their unicorn.

Babies Should Be on a Strict Schedule

Myth: If your baby isn't on a military schedule, chaos will ensue.

Reality: So you've got your baby on a schedule so precise that it would make a drill sergeant weep with pride. Diaper change at 0800, nap at 0930, and feedings every 2.35 hours. But here's the twist, babies aren't tiny soldiers. They're unpredictable little bundles of joy (and occasionally, mess). While having a routine can be helpful for establishing a sense of normalcy and predictability, it's crucial to remember that babies aren't robots programmed to follow a strict timetable. Flexibility is your secret weapon. As they grow, their needs change faster than you can say "diaper genie." One day they might need an extra nap; the next, they might want to skip it entirely and have a dance party in their crib. Babies also have their own unique rhythms. Some days, they might be hungrier than usual (hello, growth spurt!), and other days, they might need extra cuddles because they're feeling a bit off. Trying to stick to a rigid schedule during these times is like trying to stuff a wiggly octopus into a tiny box, messy and frustrating.

The key is to go with the flow. If your baby is showing signs of sleepiness, let them nap, even if it's not on the dot according to the schedule. If they're hungry, feed them, even if it's only been an hour since the last feeding. Trust your instincts and watch for your baby's cues. Being flexible doesn't mean throwing all structure out the window. You can still have a general routine, but think of it as a jazz performance rather than a military march. Improvisation is not only allowed but encouraged. You'll find that both you and your baby are happier and less stressed when you're not bound by the tyranny of the clock. So, the next time you're tempted to whip out a stopwatch at feeding time, remember: Your baby is more jazz musician than soldier. Embrace the unpredictability, and you might just enjoy the giggles, cuddles, and occasional surprises even more.

Economic Myths

Trickle-Down Economics Always Works

Myth: Give the rich more money, and they'll sprinkle it down like fairy dust.

Reality: Picture trickle-down economics like a champagne tower at a wedding. The idea is that if you pour enough champagne (money) into the top glass (the wealthy), it will overflow and fill the glasses below (everyone else). Sounds glamorous, right? But in reality, the top glass often just gets fuller and fuller, with barely a drop reaching the bottom. Here's the kicker: when wealthy folks receive more money, they don't necessarily rush out to buy more stuff like yachts or diamond-encrusted toasters. Instead, they might invest in stocks, stash it in offshore accounts, or buy up property. While these actions can grow their wealth, they don't always create jobs or boost wages for the average Joe and Jane down the economic ladder. For example, during the 1980s, the U.S. embraced trickle-down policies with tax cuts for the rich. While the stock market soared, wages for middle and lower-income workers stagnated. According to a study by the Economic Policy Institute, the wealth gap widened as the rich got richer, but the expected "trickle" to the working class was more of a dry spell. So, instead of the rich playing Santa Claus, showering us all with economic goodies, they often act more like squirrels, tucking their nuts away for winter. The lesson? A more balanced approach to economic policy, where everyone gets a fair slice of the pie, tends to work better than hoping the rich will suddenly develop a generous streak.

All Debt is Bad

Myth: Borrowing money is like making a deal with the devil

Reality: Not all debt is created equal, folks! Let's break it down; Picture debt as a tool in your financial toolbox. Good debt is like that trusty hammer you use to build a solid future, think student loans and mortgages. Student loans, for example, are like a golden ticket to higher earning potential. Sure, they might sting a bit now, but they're helping you unlock the doors to better job opportunities and higher salaries. Mortgages, on the other hand, are like planting money seeds that grow into a home sweet home tree, providing shelter and potentially appreciating in value over time. Now, let's talk about bad debt. Imagine buying a unicorn. Sounds magical, right? But do you really need a mystical creature that eats gold coins for breakfast? Bad debt is like that unicorn, tempting but not practical. This includes high-interest credit card debt or loans for luxury items that don't hold their value. You're essentially throwing money into a black hole of interest payments, which can spiral out of control faster than a toddler on a sugar rush. Here's how it works: Good debt usually has lower interest rates and longer terms, making it manageable and, ultimately, beneficial. It's like a slow-cooked stew, gradually working to nourish your financial health. Bad debt, however, comes with high interest rates and short repayment terms, much like a microwave dinner, quick but leaving you hungry and regretting your choices. To keep your financial house in order, borrow smartly. Invest in education, a home, or something that will appreciate over time or enhance your earning potential. Avoid using credit cards for splurge purchases unless you can pay them off promptly. Remember, not all debt is a one-way ticket to financial purgatory. Use it wisely, and it can be your ally rather than your nemesis.

Printing More Money Solves Economic Problems

Myth: Just print more cash! Problem solved!

Reality: If only fixing an economy was like solving a Monopoly game. Printing more money without backing it up with real value leads to inflation, which can make your hard-earned cash worth less than a banana in a monkey convention. Let's dive deeper: Imagine you're the ruler of BananaLand, where bananas are the primary currency. Life is good until one day, you decide to make everyone in BananaLand richer by printing a ton of extra bananas. "Everyone will be rich!" you declare, throwing bananas around like confetti. At first, people rejoice, building banana towers and making banana snow angels. But soon, the banana traders realize something fishy is going on. With so many bananas flooding the market, each individual banana starts losing its value. Now, instead of a car costing 100 bananas, it costs 1,000 bananas. That's inflation in action, folks! You haven't actually increased the wealth of BananaLand; you've just made bananas so common they're practically worthless. People start carrying wheelbarrows of bananas to buy groceries, and your once-celebrated banana party becomes a squishy, slippery mess. In the real world, printing more money works the same way. Money represents value, and that value comes from goods and services produced by the economy. If you print money without a corresponding increase in economic output, you're just making each dollar worth less. It's like watering down your favorite drink, it might look like you have more, but it's far less satisfying and effective. Historical case in point: Zimbabwe in the late 2000s. They printed so much money to pay off debts that hyperinflation skyrocketed. At one point, people needed trillions of Zimbabwean dollars to buy a loaf of bread. That's right, trillions! They even printed a 100 trillion dollar bill, which is great for a laugh but terrible for buying groceries. So, the next time someone suggests solving economic woes by cranking up the money printers, remind them that while it might sound like a simple solution, it's really just a fast track to making your money about as valuable as banana peels in a monkey convention.

The Stock Market Reflects the Economy

Myth: The stock market is the economy's crystal ball.

Reality: The stock market is more like the economy's mood ring, sometimes it reflects reality, sometimes it's just feeling moody. While the market can give insights, it doesn't capture the full picture of economic health, especially for everyday people who might not be invested in stocks. Alright, let's dive deeper into this colorful metaphor. Imagine the stock market as a moody teenager. One day, it's euphoric because it just got its driver's license (stock prices soaring), and the next, it's sulking because its favorite band broke up (stock prices plummeting). This volatility is often driven by investor sentiment, news headlines, and short-term events rather than the solid foundation of the economy. For example, let's say a tech company announces a new gadget. Investors might get overly excited, sending stock prices sky-high. Meanwhile, the broader economy might be struggling with unemployment or sluggish wage growth, problems that no shiny new gadget can fix.

Moreover, the stock market is a playground mainly for those who can afford to invest. According to a 2021 Gallup poll, only about

56% of Americans own stocks. That means almost half of the population is watching from the sidelines, unaffected by the market's rollercoaster ride. So, when the stock market is having a party, it doesn't mean everyone's invited. And when it's throwing a tantrum, it doesn't mean everyone's crying. Think of the economy as a big, complex machine with many moving parts: jobs, wages, production, consumption, and more. The stock market is just one flashy dial on that machine. It can tell you if investors are feeling bullish or bearish, but it can't tell you if people are finding good jobs, paying their bills, or feeling secure about their financial future. So, while the stock market can offer some clues about economic trends, relying on it to gauge the entire economy is like judging your health based solely on your mood ring. Sure, it might change color with your mood, but it won't tell you if you need a doctor's visit or if you're ready to run a marathon. In conclusion, the stock market is a fascinating part of the economic landscape, but it's not the whole picture. It's the economic equivalent of a moody teenager: insightful at times, unpredictable at others, and certainly not the ultimate authority on how everyone is really doing.

Taxes Are Always Too High

Myth: Taxes are evil, and the government is just a money vampire.

Reality: Sure, taxes aren't exactly your favorite party guests, but they're the unsung heroes of civilization. Imagine a world without them: you'd be dodging potholes the size of craters and relying on smoke signals because there'd be no 911 to call. Let's break it down: taxes fund public goods and services that everyone uses, yes, even your neighbor who never takes out their trash. These contributions build roads smoother than your best pick-up line, keep schools running so kids can learn why Pluto is no longer a planet, and ensure firefighters can rescue your cat from that very ambitious tree climb. Think of it like a giant communal pizza. Everyone chips in so we can all enjoy a slice. Without your tax dollars, we'd be fighting over crumbs. Plus, countries with higher taxes often get the deluxe pizza with extra cheese, universal healthcare, better public transportation, and more robust social services. It's like upgrading from economy to first class on a flight; yes, it costs more, but you get a lot of legroom and maybe even a complimentary drink.

So, while it might feel like your paycheck is getting nibbled on by a vampire, remember that those tax dollars are like garlic, keeping things running smoothly and saving you from a world of inconvenience. Next time you drive on a pothole-free road or enjoy a sunny day in a well-kept park, give a little nod to your taxes. They're the not-so-evil guardians of public good, keeping society from turning into a real-life episode of Survivor.

Gold is the Safest Investment

Myth: Invest in gold, and you'll be the next King Midas.

Reality: Gold is like the glittery lure at a fishing store, it looks shiny and promising, but it might not always catch the big fish. While it's true that gold can act as a safe haven during economic turbulence, like a financial security blanket, it's not the ultimate investment panacea. Here's why: Gold prices can be as moody as a teenager. They're influenced by various factors like geopolitical events, inflation rates, and even the whims of central banks. One minute it's soaring, and the next, it's as grounded as a penguin on roller skates. Unlike stocks or bonds, gold doesn't generate income. Stocks can give you dividends, and bonds pay you interest, but gold just sits there, looking pretty, waiting for the price to (hopefully) go up. Diversifying your investments is a much wiser strategy than betting everything on shiny metals. Imagine you're at a buffet. Would you only eat the glittery jello? Probably not, unless you want a very sparkly, but nutritionally void, meal. Similarly, in investing, putting all your money into gold is like making your entire meal out of
glittery jello. Sure, it looks cool, but you're missing out on all the other nutrients (or in this case, investment returns). So, while

having a bit of gold in your investment portfolio can provide stability and act as a hedge against inflation, putting all your financial eggs in the gold basket might leave you with a shiny, but unfulfilling, portfolio. Spread your investments across various asset classes, stocks, bonds, real estate, and yes, a little gold if you must, so you can enjoy a balanced and potentially more profitable financial future. Remember, even King Midas realized too much gold wasn't all it was cracked up to be!

Buying is Always Better than Renting

Myth: If you're renting, you're just throwing money away!

Reality: Owning a home sounds like the ultimate grown-up milestone, but it's not always the smartest financial move for everyone. Here's why: When you own a home, you're not just buying a cozy nest. You're also signing up for a bunch of responsibilities. Picture this: you're enjoying your Sunday, then BOOM! The water heater explodes, and now you're an unplanned contestant on "DIY Home Repair." That's right, maintenance costs, those sneaky little gremlins that keep popping up with dollar signs attached. Need a new roof? That's a small fortune. Leaky pipes? Cha-ching! Lawn needs mowing? Well, unless you fancy turning your yard into a jungle, that's more money out the door. Then there's property taxes. It's like having a subscription service for your house that you can't cancel, no matter how much you plead with customer service. These taxes can rise over time, sometimes unpredictably, like your favorite stock market meme. And let's talk about flexibility. Want to chase your dream job in another city? Love the thrill of new adventures? Renting is your best buddy. You can pack up and move with far less hassle than selling a house, which can sometimes take longer than waiting for your favorite band's reunion tour. Plus, if you're in an area where property values fluctuate more than your weight during the holidays, renting can protect you from market dips. Renting can also mean more predictable expenses. You know exactly how much you're paying each month, and when something breaks, it's the landlord's problem. Ah, sweet freedom! So, while owning a home can be wonderful, it's not the universally superior financial choice. Whether you're renting or owning, it's all about what suits your lifestyle, financial situation, and personal goals. Renting isn't "throwing money away", it's buying flexibility, peace of mind, and sometimes, just a break from the endless list of homeowner chores.

Economic Growth Can Continue Forever

Myth: The economy can grow infinitely, like your love for pizza.

Reality: Ah, if only economies were as endless as our pizza cravings. In reality, the idea that economies can expand forever without hitting any roadblocks is more fictional than unicorns juggling rainbows. Here's the scoop: economies are like roller coasters, sometimes you're climbing up, sometimes you're racing down, and occasionally, you're stuck in a loop-de-loop wondering what just happened. Economies naturally go through cycles of boom and bust. This isn't just an economic law; it's practically a fact of life, like that leftover pizza never tasting quite as good the next day. Infinite growth also overlooks a pesky little detail: finite resources. We've only got one planet, and it comes with a limited supply of goodies like oil, minerals, and even arable land. Imagine hosting a pizza party with an endless guest list but a limited number of pizzas. Sooner or later, you're going to run out of slices, and people are going to get hangry. Moreover, continuous growth can lead to serious issues like environmental degradation, social inequality, and depletion of natural resources. Think of it as eating pizza nonstop, eventually, your body will protest, and it won't be pretty. We need to focus on sustainable growth, which means finding a balance between economic development and preserving our planet. Sustainable practices, like investing in renewable energy and promoting fair trade, help ensure that we're not just gobbling up resources without a thought for the future. So, while the dream of never-ending economic expansion sounds as delicious as an infinite pizza buffet, the reality is we need to manage growth wisely. By being mindful of our resource use and focusing on sustainability, we can enjoy the economic equivalent of a balanced diet, keeping our financial systems healthy without devouring everything in sight.

Rich People Don't Pay Taxes

Myth: The rich are secret tax ninjas, dodging every fee.

Reality: Ah, the age-old myth that rich folks are all tax-evading wizards, sipping coconut water in the Bahamas while their accountants perform financial sorcery. Let's unpack this with a splash of humor and some solid facts. First off, it's true that some wealthy individuals and corporations have mastered the art of tax dodging better than Harry Houdini could escape a straitjacket. They use a combination of legal loopholes, offshore accounts, and creative accounting tricks that make a game of Twister look simple. But let's not paint everyone with the same broad brush dipped in gold. In reality, many wealthy people do pay a hefty chunk of the nation's tax bill. According to the IRS, the top 1% of earners paid about 40% of all federal income taxes in recent years. That's more than just pocket change, it's a significant contribution to public coffers. However, tax policies can sometimes feel like they were written by Rube Goldberg, making it easier for those with resources to minimize their tax liabilities. Imagine navigating a tax code that's longer than a Russian novel, filled with enough obscure deductions and credits to make your head spin faster than a merry-go-round. For example, capital gains (profits from selling assets like stocks) are often taxed at lower rates than ordinary income. This means that wealthy individuals who make most of their money through investments might pay a smaller percentage of their income in taxes compared to someone who earns a regular salary. It's like getting a discount just for playing the financial markets instead of clocking in a 9-to-5. Moreover, corporations sometimes pull off moves that would make a contortionist jealous, shifting profits to subsidiaries in low-tax countries. This practice, known as profit shifting, can lead to some eye-popping headlines about major companies paying less in taxes than you spent on your last coffee run. For instance, in 2020, 55 of America's largest companies paid $0 in federal income taxes despite collectively making billions in profits. Despite these crafty maneuvers, not all wealthy individuals are skulking around in tax havens with fake mustaches. Many pay their fair share and advocate for better tax policies to close loopholes and ensure everyone pays what they owe. They might not be volunteering to pay extra, but they're not all hiding from the IRS under a coconut tree either. In summary, while tax ninjutsu exists, and some wealthy folks are masters of the art, many still contribute significantly to the tax pool. The system could use a bit of a tune-up to ensure fairness, but let's not imagine all rich people as elusive tax-dodgers on a perpetual vacation in the tropics.

Automotive Myths

Red Cars Get More Speeding Tickets

Myth: Driving a red car is like painting a bullseye for traffic cops.

Reality: Contrary to popular belief, owning a red car doesn't turn you into an automatic magnet for speeding tickets. Studies have shown that red cars don't receive more speeding tickets than cars of any other color. Traffic cops aren't colorblind, but they're not out there playing color favorites either. Speeding tickets are based on your actual speed, not the hue of your ride. Imagine this: You're cruising in your red sports car, feeling like a superstar. Suddenly, a beige minivan zooms past you, driven by a speed demon late for soccer practice. Who gets the ticket? If the cop's radar gun says the minivan is breaking the sound barrier, the minivan driver will be the one doing the explaining. The myth likely stems from the fact that red is a flashy, attention-grabbing color. It stands out in traffic, so it's easy to assume that red cars are more noticeable and thus more likely to be pulled over. However, traffic officers rely on radar guns and their eyes on the speedometer, not a color chart. So, unless you're driving a red Ferrari at warp speed, you're as likely to get a ticket as the sensible sedan next to you.

Premium Gas Improves Performance in All Cars

Myth: Pumping premium gas will make your car feel like a racecar.

Reality: Unless your car specifically requires premium fuel, using it won't improve performance or fuel efficiency. It's like feeding a hamster caviar, it doesn't know the difference and neither does your car engine. Stick with what your owner's manual suggests. Let's delve deeper into this myth and unravel why premium gas might just be a waste of premium cash for your average ride. Premium gasoline has a higher octane rating, which means it's designed to withstand higher compression without igniting prematurely. This is essential for high-performance engines that operate under more pressure than a popcorn kernel in a microwave. However, if your car's engine is designed for regular unleaded fuel, using premium gas is about as useful as giving your pet goldfish a platinum credit card. Your engine's compression ratios aren't high enough to benefit from the extra octane, so it can't take advantage of the fuel's knock-resistance properties. It's like pouring gourmet coffee into a regular drip machine, it's not going to taste any different from the regular stuff. Manufacturers design most car engines to run efficiently on regular unleaded gas. They meticulously calibrate the engine's timing and fuel injection to optimize performance for the specified octane level. When you pour in premium fuel, your car's computer might not even realize it's sipping on the fancy stuff and will just keep running as usual. So, unless you've got a sports car with a high-compression engine that demands premium, you're essentially throwing money into the gas tank without seeing any tangible benefits. In fact, the only thing that might go faster is your wallet's departure from your pocket. So, the next time you're at the pump, remember: your trusty sedan isn't living a secret double life as a race car. Save the extra bucks for something more rewarding, like a nice treat for yourself (or your hamster, if it really likes caviar). In summary, follow your owner's manual like it's a GPS leading you to savings and engine happiness. Regular gas is perfectly fine for most cars, and premium gas, well, that's just a premium myth for most of us.

SUVs Are Safer Than Smaller Cars

Myth: Bigger is always better when it comes to car safety.

Reality: Ah, the mighty SUV, the king of the road, the tank of the suburbs. You might think that driving a vehicle the size of a small house means you're cruising around in a fortress of invincibility. But hold your horses, this myth needs a pit stop for some truth. Sure, SUVs can offer more protection in certain types of collisions. When you're sitting high and mighty, surrounded by metal and airbags, you might feel like nothing can touch you. But here's the plot twist: SUVs have a pesky little problem called rollover risk. With a higher center of gravity, these giants are more prone to tipping over, especially if you take that corner like you're in a high-speed chase scene. Meanwhile, modern small cars have been hitting the gym. They're now packed with advanced safety features that could make a bodyguard jealous. We're talking about anti-lock brakes, electronic stability control, and more airbags than a balloon factory. Some even come with collision avoidance systems that practically have a sixth sense.

Manual Transmissions Get Better Fuel Economy

Myth: Shifting gears manually saves you a fortune on gas.

Reality: Buckle up, because the days of manual transmissions being the fuel economy champs are as outdated as flip phones. Modern automatic transmissions have evolved into gear-shifting wizards, often matching or even surpassing their manual counterparts in fuel efficiency. Thanks to advancements like continuously variable transmissions (CVTs) and dual-clutch systems, your car's onboard computer now shifts gears with the precision of a Swiss watchmaker. While Aunt Mabel might have mastered the art of smooth gear transitions on a leisurely Sunday drive, today's automatic transmissions are designed to optimize every drop of fuel. They adapt to driving conditions in real-time, ensuring you're always in the right gear for maximum efficiency. Imagine having a tiny automotive engineer living under your hood, constantly tweaking your transmission for peak performance. That's what modern automatics do!

You Should Warm Up Your Car Before Driving

Myth: Your car needs a good stretch before it hits the road.

Reality: Modern engines are built to leap into action almost immediately. Idling your car in the driveway is more about wasting gas than warming up the engine. Just take it easy for the first few minutes of driving, and your car will thank you. Let's dive deeper, shall we? Back in the days when mullets were in style and cars had carburetors, warming up your engine before driving was as essential as a good mixtape. But guess what? Times have changed, and so have engines! Today's cars come equipped with electronic fuel injection and advanced technology that makes idling for long periods as outdated as those leg warmers in your closet. Here's how it works: modern engines are designed to reach optimal operating temperature quickly and efficiently. When you start your car, the engine management system kicks in and starts adjusting fuel and air mixtures on the fly, ensuring your engine warms up as you drive. Think of it like your car saying, *"Hey, I'm good to go! Let's hit the road together."*
Idling not only wastes fuel but also increases emissions, bad for your wallet and the planet. Plus, prolonged idling can actually

cause engine components to wear out faster. It's like making your car run in place on a treadmill while you wait for it to break a sweat. Spoiler alert: it doesn't need to! So next time you're tempted to sit in the driveway, waiting for your car to get its metaphorical morning coffee, just remember: a gentle drive is all it needs to wake up. Your car isn't a lazy teenager, it's more like a well-trained athlete, ready to perform without the long warm-up. Drive gently for the first few minutes, and both you and your engine will be happier and healthier in the long run.

Controversial Myths

Vaccines Cause Autism

Myth: Vaccines are plotting with autism to take over the world.

Reality: This myth began with a debunked study by Andrew Wakefield in 1998, which has since been thoroughly discredited. Extensive research shows no link between vaccines and autism. Vaccines are essential for public health, preventing diseases like measles, mumps, and whooping cough. Alright, let's dive deeper; Imagine the world of vaccines as a bustling superhero headquarters. Each vaccine has its own superpower: the measles vaccine can fend off that pesky virus, the mumps vaccine packs a punch against swollen glands, and the whooping cough vaccine stops those coughs that sound like a goose with a megaphone. These heroes are here to protect us, not to plot world domination with autism. The myth that vaccines cause autism originated from a study led by Andrew Wakefield in 1998. This study claimed a link between the MMR (measles, mumps, rubella) vaccine and autism. However, this research was about as legitimate as a three-dollar bill. Wakefield's study had a sample size smaller than a pizza party, used flawed methods, and was funded by parties with financial interests in lawsuits against vaccine manufacturers. Basically, it was the research equivalent of a high school rumor gone wild. Fast forward to today, and Wakefield's study has been thoroughly discredited and retracted. Multiple large-scale studies involving hundreds of thousands of children have found no connection between vaccines and autism. None. Zilch. Nada. If vaccines and autism were characters in a buddy cop movie, they'd be the duo that never met. Here's how vaccines really work: When you get vaccinated, you're essentially giving your immune system a mugshot of the bad guy (the virus). Your body then learns how to recognize and defeat it without getting sick. It's like a training montage in a superhero movie, by the time the real villain shows up, your immune system is ready to kick butt and take names. Meanwhile, the supposed villain, autism, is a complex neurodevelopmental disorder that researchers believe is primarily influenced by genetics and some environmental factors. It's not lurking in your vaccine vial, waiting to pounce. The rise in autism diagnoses is more likely due to better awareness and diagnostic criteria, not because vaccines are up to no good. The importance of vaccines cannot be overstated. They've helped eradicate smallpox, nearly eliminated polio, and significantly reduced the incidence of many other infectious diseases. Thanks to vaccines, we're not dealing with outbreaks of diseases that used to cause widespread suffering and death. In conclusion, vaccines aren't plotting with autism, they're busy saving the world, one shot at a time.

Climate Change is a Hoax

Myth: Climate change is just Mother Nature having a hot flash.

Reality: Let's face it, Mother Nature isn't going through menopause, and she certainly isn't having a cosmic hot flash. The overwhelming majority of scientists (we're talking about 97% of them) agree that climate change is real and primarily driven by human activities, like burning fossil fuels. Ignoring it won't make it go away, just like ignoring your laundry pile won't magically clean your clothes. But let's dive deeper into this hot topic, shall we? First, a quick science lesson: The Earth's atmosphere is like a big, cozy blanket. It keeps us warm by trapping heat from the sun. This is called the greenhouse effect, and it's a good thing, without it, we'd be popsicles. But here's the catch: when we burn fossil fuels (coal, oil, natural gas), we release carbon dioxide (CO_2) and other greenhouse gases into the atmosphere. This is like adding extra layers to our blanket until we're sweating buckets in the middle of the night. Think of CO_2 as the overzealous roommate who keeps cranking up the thermostat. The more CO_2 we pump into the atmosphere, the thicker our blanket gets, trapping more heat and causing global temperatures to rise. This leads to a host of issues, from melting ice caps and rising sea levels to extreme weather events and disrupted ecosystems. It's not just about warmer winters, climate change can throw everything out of whack, like trying to play Jenga during an earthquake. To put it in perspective, the past decade was the hottest on record. Glaciers are retreating faster than your hairline, sea levels are rising like a soufflé, and extreme weather events are becoming as common as cat videos on the internet. And just like that laundry pile, the longer we ignore it, the bigger the mess we'll have to clean up later. But don't just take my word for it. Scientists have been studying climate change for decades, using everything from ice core samples to satellite data. They've built sophisticated models that predict future climate scenarios, and the consensus is clear: we need to act now to reduce our greenhouse gas emissions and mitigate the impacts of climate change. Think of it as cleaning your room before your mom comes over, it's a lot easier to maintain than to deal with the aftermath of neglect. So next time someone tells you climate change is a hoax, remember this: the science is solid, the evidence is overwhelming, and Mother Nature isn't just having a hot flash. She's sending us a wake-up call, and it's high time we hit the snooze button and got to work. Otherwise, we'll be left sweating under a blanket we can't kick off.

5G Technology Causes Health Issues

Myth: 5G towers are zapping us into zombies.

Reality: Picture this: You're walking down the street, minding your own business, when a 5G tower suddenly zaps you into a mindless, Wi-Fi-craving zombie. Sounds like a plot from a B-rated sci-fi movie, right? That's because it is, there's no real-life science supporting this electrifying myth. First, let's get a bit technical but not too boring, I promise! 5G stands for the fifth generation of mobile network technology, promising us faster internet speeds, more reliable connections, and the ability to stream cat videos in HD with zero buffering. The radiofrequency waves used in 5G are non-ionizing, meaning they don't have enough energy to remove tightly bound electrons or alter DNA. They're the friendly waves, like those used in your TV and microwave, not the villainous ones like X-rays. Think of it this way: If 5G waves were people, they'd be the chill surfers hanging out on the beach, not the overzealous gym buffs lifting weights. Non-ionizing radiation from 5G can't cause cancer or fry your brain cells because it lacks the power to mess with your molecular structure.

Numerous studies and health organizations, including the World Health Organization (WHO) and the International Commission on Non-Ionizing Radiation Protection (ICNIRP), have concluded that 5G technology is safe. They've looked at the evidence, scratched their heads, and said, "Nope, no zombies here." Moreover, 5G technology actually uses lower power levels compared to previous generations. Imagine your old 4G phone was a boombox blasting music at full volume, while your new 5G phone is a Bluetooth speaker playing smooth jazz. It's quieter, more efficient, and less likely to annoy your neighbors, or your cells. But wait, there's more! The radiofrequency exposure from 5G is significantly lower than what you get from other everyday sources, like your microwave or even the sun. In conclusion, while 5G is revolutionizing our internet experience, it's not turning us into zombies or causing mysterious health issues. It's just making our devices faster and our lives a bit more convenient. So, next time you see a 5G tower, give it a friendly wave and enjoy the seamless connectivity. The only thing it's zapping is your buffering time.

The Earth is Flat

Myth: The Earth is flatter than a pancake.

Reality: The Earth is round, as proven by countless scientific observations and space missions. If the Earth were flat, cats would have knocked everything off the edge by now. But let's dig into this a bit more with a pinch of humor and a heap of science. First, let's address the pancake analogy. If the Earth were truly as flat as a pancake, we'd have more pressing concerns, like syrupy oceans and butter mountains. But in reality, Earth is an oblate spheroid, meaning it's mostly round but slightly squished at the poles and bulging at the equator. Imagine a squishy beach ball someone sat on, still round, but with a bit of character. One of the simplest pieces of evidence for a round Earth is the horizon. Ever noticed how ships seem to sink into the sea as they sail away? They're not disappearing off the edge; they're gradually going over the curvature of the Earth. If you still think they're falling off a giant pancake, then it's time to upgrade your view. Next up, gravity. On a flat Earth, gravity would pull everything toward the center of the disc, making life a bit like a wonky carnival ride. We'd all be sliding toward the middle, and living on the edges would be like trying to walk uphill all the time. Thank goodness we live on a round planet where gravity pulls us nicely towards the center, keeping everything grounded.

Let's talk about travel. If you've ever flown long distances, you've likely experienced the joy of crossing time zones. On a flat Earth, time zones would be a chaotic mess, with noon happening simultaneously everywhere or not at all. It would be like trying to use a single clock to schedule a global pizza party, utterly impossible. The round Earth explains why it's sunny in New York while people in Tokyo are counting sheep. Space missions provide some of the most concrete evidence. Thousands of photos from space show our beautiful blue planet in all its spherical glory. If you believe the Earth is flat, you'd have to think that every astronaut, scientist, and satellite engineer is part of an elaborate prank. And honestly, who has time for that? They're busy exploring the universe, not staging a cosmic comedy show. Finally, there's the cat test. If the Earth were flat, cats would have pushed everything off the edge by now. These furry chaos agents can't resist knocking things over, and if there were an edge, they'd find it. Since we're not living in a world constantly losing its keys and coffee mugs to the abyss, it's safe to say our planet is round. So, while the idea of a flat Earth might be an entertaining plot for a sci-fi novel, the reality is much more spherical. Embrace the roundness and enjoy knowing that wherever you stand, you're part of a giant, spinning ball in space.

Homeopathy is Effective

Myth: Diluting something a billion times makes it super powerful.

Reality: Imagine if the secret to curing your cold was to take one drop of medicine, drop it into the Atlantic Ocean, and then scoop up a glass to drink. Congratulations, you've just made a homeopathic remedy! Homeopathy operates on the principle of "like cures like," meaning if something causes symptoms in a healthy person, a very diluted version of that same thing can cure similar symptoms in a sick person. The problem? These dilutions are so extreme that you're more likely to find a needle in a haystack than a single molecule of the original substance in the remedy. Here's how it works (or doesn't): A substance is diluted in water or alcohol, and then shaken vigorously. This process is repeated multiple times, sometimes until there's practically no chance that even one molecule of the original substance remains. It's like making a margarita, but after you've added the tequila, you dump it into a pool, stir, take a drop from the pool, and then pour that drop into another pool. By the time you're done, you're essentially just drinking pool water.

Proponents of homeopathy claim that water has a "memory" and remembers what was once in it, kind of like how you remember that embarrassing thing you did in fifth grade. But unlike your brain, water doesn't have a memory. If it did, it'd be remembering all sorts of things, fish, algae, and that time someone peed in the ocean. Scientific studies have shown that homeopathy is no more effective than a placebo. In other words, taking a homeopathic remedy is about as effective as wishing really hard that you'll get better. Your brain might trick you into feeling a bit better, but it's not the diluted water doing the magic, it's your mind. If you're sick, stick to treatments backed by science. Real medicine is tested rigorously, like a superhero going through training montages, to ensure it's safe and effective. Homeopathy, on the other hand, is more like a well-dressed imposter at the superhero convention. It might look convincing at first, but it doesn't have the superpowers to back it up.

The Moon Landing Was Faked

Myth: The moon landing was a Hollywood production.

Reality: Let's tackle this one giant leap for myth-busting, shall we? Some folks believe the moon landing was a cinematic masterpiece, directed by Stanley Kubrick, with a budget bigger than "2001: A Space Odyssey." But here's why this idea is more far-fetched than a moon made of cheese. First off, the 1969 moon landing by NASA's Apollo 11 mission was as real as Neil Armstrong's iconic footprint. We've got rock-solid evidence, literally. The Apollo missions brought back 382 kilograms (about 842 pounds) of moon rocks. These aren't your garden-variety rocks; they've been studied by scientists worldwide, confirming their extraterrestrial origin. If Hollywood could fake that, they'd be the true masters of special effects. Then there are the photos and videos. Critics argue about shadows and flag flutters, but these can be explained by basic physics and the unique environment of the moon. No atmosphere means no wind resistance, so when astronauts planted the flag, it waved because of inertia. And the lighting? Multiple light sources, including the sun and the reflective lunar surface, create those odd shadows.

Alexander C.

Sorry, conspiracy theorists, but even Kubrick couldn't defy the laws of physics. And let's not forget the equipment left behind. From lunar modules to retroreflectors used to measure the distance between Earth and the moon, these items are still there. Amateur astronomers and even high-powered telescopes can spot them, providing a visual reminder that we were there. It's like leaving your toys in the sandbox and being able to see them from your bedroom window. Now, consider the sheer number of people involved in the Apollo program, around 400,000 engineers, scientists, and support staff. Expecting all of them to keep such a monumental secret? That's like trying to stop a cat from knocking things off the table, impossible. Secrets that big would have leaked faster than a sieve in a waterfall. Plus, other countries, like the Soviet Union, were monitoring the mission closely. If there had been any funny business, they would have been the first to blow the whistle, not quietly watch their space-race rivals bask in unearned glory. So, unless you believe in a global conspiracy involving thousands of people, complex scientific hoaxes, and international cooperation worthy of an Olympic medal, it's safe to say the moon landing was as real as it gets. Buzz Aldrin didn't punch a moon landing denier just for fun, he did it because sometimes, the truth needs a solid right hook!

And there you have it, an epic journey through the world of myths, misconceptions, and downright funky fallacies! From the deepest corners of space to the quirkiest corners of your kitchen, we've debunked the myths that have been pulling the wool over our eyes for far too long. But remember, dear reader, this book isn't just about setting the record straight; it's about empowering you with knowledge. Armed with these truths, you're now ready to challenge the next dubious factoid that comes your way. Whether it's over a dinner table debate or a friendly trivia night, you'll be the go-to myth-buster, dazzling your friends with both wit and wisdom. So, what's next? Keep questioning, keep exploring, and most importantly, keep laughing. The world is full of mysteries and misunderstandings just waiting to be unraveled. Approach them with curiosity and a healthy dose of skepticism. After all, the truth is out there, sometimes you just have to dig through a pile of myths to find it. Thank you for joining me on this myth-busting adventure. I hope you had as much fun reading as I did writing it. Remember, knowledge is power, and a good laugh is the best companion on any journey. Now go forth, debunk, and spread the truth! Until our next adventure,

Alexander C

Printed in Great Britain
by Amazon